DON'T WAIT CREATE

ERIKA MCCALL

CONTENTS

INTRODUCTION

It's 2010, and I'm standing in the kitchen reading the unedited manuscript of my debut book *Go for Yours*, to my mother and grandmother. *"So, what does it mean to Go for Yours? Some call it grinding; others call it hustling. No matter the case, to Go for Yours means you don't wait on an opportunity—you create it."*

I began to envision myself at the local bookstore, reading to a supportive audience. As I finish my sentence, both start to clap, telling me how much they enjoyed the words typed on twenty pages. My grandmother grabs the short manuscript and begins to pray, *"Lord take it higher, and higher, and higher."* At that moment, none of us was aware of the journey ahead. We had no idea that the words I had just shared would one day turn into a business, brand, and nonprofit foundation, among other things. We were just enjoying a moment together. We were three generations of women, who at the time hadn't realized all that would manifest because of prayer.

Over ten years later and I am still trying to fathom where my journey has brought me. It's hard to believe when just a decade ago, I was living in my grandmother's basement in Chicago with a limited vision of what was in store for my future. At that time, I wanted to publish a book but was oblivious to the process. Not to mention, I had a full-time job. When would I have time to complete this book? Maybe it's just a pipe dream. These are thoughts that crept through my mind from time to time. My mindset began to shift when I witnessed what was supposed to be a book of quotes turn into a compilation of stories about young people who are brave enough to step out on faith and reach for the stars. The people I met and interviewed during this process were extraordinary. Instead of focusing on my lack of knowledge, I tapped into my faith and believed if God did something miraculous for them, He could do the same for me.

Today, I'm sitting in my one-bedroom apartment in North Hollywood, California, as a published author and business owner. Once again, I envision myself in front of an audience reading *Don't Wait, Create*. This time, on a 10-city book tour to a crowd filled with new and familiar faces. As I continue to imagine all the places and experiences my journey will continue to bring, I look forward to hearing about all of the creative projects birthed by the people who read this book.

While anticipating all the lives that will be touched, I can't help but think about whose life my journey has impacted the most. That person is me. After deciding to begin creating opportunities I had been waiting for, I met a brand-new person that had been lingering inside of me. In my first book, I hid my story behind all the people I was featuring. It wasn't until after publishing *Go for Yours* that I realized how impactful my story was. I am most excited to provide you with my authentic story to help you birth whatever vision that is resting in your soul. I genuinely believe that you possess everything you need to bring all your dreams to fruition.

Honestly, I have been sitting on this book for over three years. Can you believe that someone who encourages people to create instead of wait did the same thing? Thankfully, God's timing is perfect. If I had published this book prematurely, it wouldn't have done you or me any justice. Within the last three years, I learned more strategies to help you during your creation process. As you move forward in this book, you will become knowledgeable about practical tools to help you create opportunities to live out your God-given purpose. Please pay close attention as I use my experiences to elaborate on key concepts and messages that will help you jumpstart whatever you were born to create.

During our time together, grab your Don't Wait Create journal and start thinking about what dream you are ready to bring to life. Whatever it is, I pray the same prayer my grandmother prayed. Like my dream, I pray yours goes higher, higher, and higher. Let's get to creating!

CALLED TO CREATE

*"For we are God's handiwork, created in Christ Jesus to do good
works, which God prepared in advance for us to do.*
—Ephesians 2:10

Y ou were created with intention. You were created
with a purpose. You were created to CREATE.
Your arrival on earth was not by mistake. When I think
about all of the relationships that led to us being here, it
blows my mind. Think about it, not only did our parents
have to meet, but their parents, your great-grandparents,
and so on. You, my friend, were intentionally designed
for a time such as this. It's time to stop waiting for a
miracle to happen before you start creating. You are the
MIRACLE that has already happened. In the words of
Nike, JUST DO IT!

Imagine you have an incoming phone call, and it's
God on the other end. You pick up, and He gives you a

specific assignment only you can accomplish. You don't have all of the instructions but special abilities to complete the mission. It may not be in the form of a call or text, but the ideas tugging at your heart, keeping you up at night is God calling you to create. Your gifts, skills, and talents are the superpowers He has given you to carry out your vision.

When I fully embraced that God created me for a particular purpose, I began to live my dream confidently. Once you accept your calling, you won't feel like you are following a dream. It will be the exact opposite. The world around you will begin to change, and your dreams will start to follow you. Within you, you have the power to create something that could potentially change the world, shift culture, or save lives. The time to do it is now.

I went through a period in my life when I felt like I was on the outside looking into people's lives that have unleashed their power. The people I learned about while writing *Go for Yours* created the types of opportunities that most people sit and wait for. As I observed, I watched people fulfill dreams with confidence, allowing nothing to stand in the way. Curiosity made me test my observations and join a unique group of individuals who have created a lifestyle filled with purpose. When I put away my old way of thinking and moved in the direction I was being called to, the world around me began to change.

I discovered a rare group of innovative leaders who merge their ideas with technology, education, or any resource to help them leave a lasting impact on the earth. They worked hard, yet smart, and were willing to go the extra mile most aren't willing to. Some wake up at the crack of dawn to work on a new project, while others wait until the sun goes down to bring forth their ideas. One thing that stood out was the fact that they defined success on their own terms.

Some of the people I encountered were climbing up the ranks in Silicon Valley, while others were developing a blueprint in their parent's garage. A few of them spent numerous hours in the studio, creating music that will eventually shift the culture. I even met some in middle school, high school, and college preparing to become the next powerful attorney, physician, teacher, or whatever they have set their mind to do. There were several whose future depended on their next slam dunk, home run, touchdown, or tennis match. All had different desires but similar qualities that make them stand out in a world where most people are afraid to do something extraordinary.

I have met so many exceptional individuals from various cultures and backgrounds, but all have one thing in common: the desire to create something well beyond their imagination. The most significant discovery was to find out that I possessed similar qualities. The dream that felt so far away was waiting on me to realize the supernatural powers intentionally downloaded into my DNA to carry out God's plans for my life. That miraculous power took me from being a shy girl who was raised in the midst of cornfields and told she was a horrible writer to a confident woman who has embraced everything she is being called to be and has broken many barriers.

There is no doubt in my mind that you are one of the unique individuals I just described. You have a special gift ready to make room for you as soon as you decide to create rather than wait. If you are having a hard time believing me, it's okay. I have done the dirty work. Only to come back and tell you that you have everything you need to begin your creative journey. Grab your Don't Wait Create journal and answer the following questions.

1. What do you believe you are being called to create?
2. How will the world be impacted by what you decide to create?

DON'T WAIT

"Good things come to those who wait, not to those who wait too late."
—Bill Withers, *Just the Two of Us*

WAIT
verb (used with object)

1. to continue as one is in expectation of; *to wait for one's turn at a telephone booth.*

verb (used without object)

1. to stay where one is or delaying action until a particular time or until something else happens.

M ost of us are sitting on talents that God intended for us to use. Although I am no longer sleeping on my gifts, I use the term "us" because if my fellow creative geniuses are not operating in their true callings, I want to do my part to bring about some change. It's easy to think that we will fulfill our calling "one day" when the time is right. Leaving us to wait instead of hitting the ground running.

The definitions at the beginning of this chapter describe two forms of waiting. I want to explore both because there will be times when you have no other choice but to wait. We wait for our turn in the check-out line, our rideshare to arrive, or a movie to start in our daily lives. In more serious instances, we wait until we have completed the required courses to graduate, meet the right person to get married or have enough money saved to take a trip out of the country. This type of waiting is active and intentional.

I am speaking to the stagnant people that delay action until something other than themselves comes to help them achieve their goals. For every person I have met that is operating in their true calling, I have met seven who are waiting on an outside factor to pursue what is already available to them. The most popular form of delay comes from waiting for people to give us permission to follow our dream or provide us with an opportunity. This type of waiting is the quickest way to rob yourself of what you were born to achieve. It's toxic and will steal your joy, leaving you to feel defeated, depressed and hopeless. How do I know? Well, it almost happened to me.

A few months before reading my manuscript in the kitchen, I was on a flight, 30,000 feet in the air traveling from Atlanta to Chicago. I had just finished bringing in the New Year with my line sister, Tiara. Together, we declared that our year would be like none other we have ever experienced. Typically, flights coming back from a festive weekend consisted of on and off naps until I landed. This flight was different. As I sat on the plane, I began to write quotes in my journal. One of them being *Go for Yours*. I have loved this phrase since the very first time I heard it from my good friend Anthony "Ant P" Peterson while in college. He was trying to convince me to make a move on my crush by telling me, *Go for Yours*. I didn't take his advice at that particular moment, but the words always stuck with me. By the end of the flight, I had made up my mind. That year, I would write a book, and it would be titled *Go for Yours*.

Initially, my idea was a coffee table book filled with quotes and examples of young people who modeled them. As I continued to write, my vision grew. The small paragraphs typed in my Google drive turned into pages highlighting the accomplishments of people who served as an example of everything I was documenting. The thought of publishing became a strong passion, but something held me back from fully committing myself to my newly found dream. The obstacle that stood in between me and my vision was my full-time employment.

Fresh out of graduate school, I had landed a job at a private university in Chicago as the Assistant Director of Diversity & Leadership. I loved everything about my position because it allowed me to work with talented young people who were excited about their future. Before receiving my master's degree in Higher

Education, I was working in the field of Social Work. As a case manager, my job was to reunite families who fell victim to the foster care system. This career didn't last long because it was challenging for me to work with people who didn't seem to want my help.

Finally, I had a job that would jumpstart my career while providing me with my own office, salary, and benefits. In my mid-twenties, with very few responsibilities, this position contributed to my plan of living the adult lifestyle I had envisioned for myself. In the next couple of years, I would be able to do things people in their late twenties did, like purchase a home, start a family, and work my way up to an executive position. To facilitate my action plan and save money, I moved into a small room in my grandmother's basement.

As excited as I was about my new passion, it was not enough to make me leave a job that provided me with financial security. Therefore, I decided to wait a little longer, write in my spare time and save money to publish my book. Writing became my "dream on the side." After work, and sometimes on the weekend, I would sit at home for hours writing and creating story concepts. Eventually, my dedication to creating *Go for Yours* became so strong that it became a significant part of my life. When students come to my office in need of encouragement, I would refer to some of the stories I was developing in my book.

When summer approached, my job became so demanding that I didn't have time to write. On top of that, my supervisors began to micromanage me and put me on a six-month Performance Improvement Plan (PIP) because they felt I wasn't performing up to their expectations. Being micromanaged shifted my focus to dedicating my time to keeping my job and improving my performance to prove that I was an exceptional employee.

That same summer, I took a trip to New Orleans to attend my sorority's national convention. When packing my bags, I noticed a year-old copy of *Black Enterprise* sitting on the coffee table that I had only used for decoration. I grabbed it so I could have something to read on the plane. Again, 30,000 feet in the air, I became inspired while reading the articles in the magazine about young entrepreneurs who created their very own opportunity for success. I read in amazement about Jerome Boykin, who, at the age of 23, started a parking lot cleaning business after he lost all his belongings in Hurricane Katrina. Jerome made $850,000 in revenues his first year in business, eventually becoming a millionaire. I also read about siblings Lorielle and Brandon Broussard. Together, they started Barackawear, a t-shirt company, and created Barack the Vote t-shirts to support President-elect Barack Obama's 2008 election campaign.

When I returned to Chicago, I sent Jerome Boykin an email informing him I was inspired by his story and wanted to interview him for my book. A few days later, Jerome contacted me, letting me know he received my message. He said he usually didn't get a chance to call people because of his busy schedule, but my email stood out to him. Jerome was the very first person I interviewed and encouraged me along the way of completing *Go for Yours*. Interviewing Jerome inspired me to seek more personal stories. I discovered so many influential trailblazers who had great stories of success.

Another one of my favorite stories was about Kari Miller, who I had become familiar with after researching people with triumphant stories. Kari became a Gold Medalist after losing her limbs in a horrific car accident. It wasn't until she experienced this accident that she learned how to play volleyball. I remember reflecting on all the powerful stories that would motivate my readers and inspire them to be confident enough to pursue a crazy idea or passion.

Closer to the finish line, it was time to provide a brief synopsis of my book. I leaned into some friends to help me come up with the perfect description. *"Go for Yours, a guide for ambitious, faithful, and progressive individuals who yearn to break the conventional models of living."* I was about to publish a book encouraging people to do something brave while doing the exact opposite. Highlighting all of these amazing individuals made me question the real reason I was waiting so long to do what was tugging at my heart. Deep down in my spirit, I knew this book would take me beyond having my own office and climbing up the ranks in my career. I was heading to a place where there were no limits to how far I could go. Still, there was something subconsciously preventing me from moving forward in the direction I was yearning to go. I really wanted to leave my job to see where my vision would take me, but the thought of being broke and never making it out of my grandmother's basement stopped me right in my tracks.

By the end of the year, *Go for Yours* came to a standstill. Publishing was still in my plans, but I didn't have a real deadline. On one of the coldest days of the year, I was in the house watching Kimora Lee Simmons' *Life in the Fab Lane.* She was somewhere in Los Angeles, at a restaurant, sitting outside under the sun, at a business meeting with her shades on. I recalled the team meeting I had earlier in the day that took place in a small and stuffy conference room. I began to envision myself creating my own schedule, taking meetings outside in the warm weather, and actively living my dream, making real boss moves. I felt like *Go for Yours* was the key that would open new doors. I don't know if it was the stillness of the winter or the lack of sunshine, but at that moment, my dream couldn't have seemed further away. My present condition made it hard for me to see what was right in front of me.

A few weeks later, I was heading to work during the first big snowstorm of the year. I couldn't help but think about what life would be like if I decided to follow what had been continuously tugging at my heart. I dug my car out of the snow, warmed it up, and headed to work. When I arrived, there was an email from my supervisor requesting a meeting to review my PIP. Before heading to her office, I opened my desk drawer and grabbed the letter of resignation that had been sitting there for months. I didn't know what it would lead to, but it was time for me to live out everything I was writing about and finish my project. In my meeting, I provided my supervisor with two weeks' notice. She asked me to leave that day.

I will never forget the disrespect I experienced while packing up my office. I called two of my friends and asked them to help me clean out my office. While gathering my items, we could hear my supervisor and the Dean of Students laughing and talking about what was taking place. As we closed the last box and went to grab the flash drive from my computer, the Dean entered the office, snatched the flash drive out of my hand, and accused me of trying to steal the university's files. I still have no idea why she would think I wanted any of their files, but the adrenaline in my body caused me to snatch my flash drive back from her. She could have everything else, but on that flash drive was my manuscript and the key that would open the door for what was lying ahead.

As I reflect on the events that led to the decision to follow my dream, I can't help but think about why it took me so long to leave a job that didn't value me. In hindsight, I was too scared to break a tradition that encourages you to obtain a degree, get a job, start a family, and retire—in that order.

For years, hundreds of thousands of people have been pursuing dreams based on society's standard of living. Instead of defining it on their own terms, they have measured their success based on others' opinions. My experience has taught me, there is nothing wrong with achieving the goals mentioned above, but it shouldn't be based on the world's terms. It's okay to start a family before tackling your professional goals. Or put your personal goals on hold to achieve professionally. You can also pursue everything you want at the same time. It's your life, and you only get one.

More than ever, people are breaking conventional living models and refusing to be put in a box. They don't even believe there is a box. But for every person shattering boxes and creating their own path, there is someone stuck on a more comfortable and safer route waiting for the perfect time or circumstance to pursue what is truly in their hearts. Too many people are living an unhappy mediocre life because they are afraid. Instead, they water down their vision to fit in with the traditional idea of how they think life should be lived. I can say without hesitation that deciding to create *Go for Yours* saved my life. It helped me discover my purpose and provided me with many experiences filled with lesson after lesson. Despite the accomplishments, there is a possibility that I would be further along in my journey if I hadn't waited. Now it's time for you to stop waiting. Grab your journal and answer the following questions.

1. Based on the definitions of waiting, are you actively or passively pursuing your passion?
2. What is the number one thing making you wait?
3. Is there a job or responsibility that is making it hard to find time to pursue your passion?

TWO TYPES OF CREATORS

JOB

noun

1. A piece of work, especially a specific task done as part of the routine of one's occupation or for an agreed price.

PURPOSE

noun

1. The reason for which something exists or is done, made, used, etc.

Everyone's story of discovering their purpose will be different. My journey of creating resulted in me leaving my full-time job to tend to the gifts God placed inside of me. But this may not apply to everyone.

Some of you will fulfill your purpose while having a full-time job, and others won't. I am not here to encourage you to quit your job in exchange for being your own boss. It's about identifying your gifts and finding opportunities to share your light with the world.

Many of us have struggled to discover our real purpose because we think it correlates with what we do for a living. If your job doesn't seem as valuable as one that appears more prestigious, it could make you feel like you have no meaning. This is dangerous because although our jobs play a role in our journey, it's not what makes us unique.

A job is a means to an end; your purpose is the reason you exist. It has the final say. If you leave a place of employment, your purpose goes with you. It doesn't stay with the job you once had. After Geoffrey Owens, who is known for his role as Alvin on the *Cosby Show*, was seen at the local Trader Joe's bagging groceries, people's first reaction was that he had hit rock bottom. The world of social media went crazy and began to job shame Geoffrey while circulating his picture around the internet. He quickly let the world know that no one should feel sorry for him. He had a great job with benefits. Geoffrey was able to happily bag groceries because he knew his current position did not take away from his purpose.

No matter how high you feel your calling is, there may be times when you have to take a job just to keep the lights on. Geoffrey is the perfect example that your job is not the same as your purpose. His understanding of this is what has resulted in him being busy and booked. He went from bagging groceries in Trader Joes to being back on the television and movie screen. People admired his dedication and wanted to support his Hollywood endeavors.

When you are connected to your calling, you won't feel too good to take a job that is going to help you with your overall goals. I have taken on many odd jobs with my goal in mind, including driving for Lyft, electronic court reporting, and renting my apartment out on Airbnb. These jobs helped me stay afloat while building my foundation and working on various projects. When I was driving for Lyft, and some of my passengers told me I reminded them of Issa from *Insecure*, whose character drove for the same company and worked for a nonprofit, We Got Y'all, I didn't take it personally. Instead of feeling "insecure" or embarrassed, I reminded myself that my side gigs contributed to my goals. A job could be the very thing that helps you step into the next dimension of your life.

Also, be mindful that before God elevates you, he may put you in certain situations to prepare you for your blessing. If you were to receive the blessing automatically, you may not have developed the character you would have built driving for Lyft or working at the local restaurant. Every experience, trial, and tribulation plays a role in your purpose. We will dive more into that later.

Being connected to what God intended for you to do won't allow you to take a job just because of money. You will be able to properly evaluate how it fits in with your goals, morals, and vision. You won't be so quick to take it just because it is a means to an end. If you are suddenly let go from a job or demoted, you won't confuse it with losing purpose. You will have the full understanding that God is your provider, and He will provide you with everything you need.

Now that you understand your job does not determine your purpose, you can begin exploring ways to step into it fully. It could be through the work you do or extracurricular activities. Whatever you decide, just remember your purpose goes wherever you go. Taking all of this into consideration, you have two types of creators. The 9-5 with a creative side, and then you have the entrepreneur who creates a job for themselves and may take a few side gigs.

9-5 With A Creative Side

A demanding job can make it difficult to nurture the creativity waiting to burst. Team meetings, deadlines, and long hours will leave you feeling drained when you finally have time to tend to the creative juices flowing in your brain. With entrepreneurship on the rise, traditional jobs are becoming less appealing. More than half of millennials classify themselves as entrepreneurs. In a study conducted by Universum Global, they found that 36% of Generation Z fear that they will be stuck in careers that do not allow them to develop opportunities. My friends in the traditional workplace often share their frustrations of having a 9 to 5.

If you are becoming fed up with your job, I have

some advice for you, stay as long as you can. I know, I know! I sound like I'm contradicting myself. But as someone who left a job on a whim, there are some things I would have done differently. Thankfully, I had very little responsibility. I encourage you to be strategic in your leap of faith if you have various commitments. Unless you know it's the Holy Spirit telling you to move right away, don't make a move until you begin creating a strategy. If I could change things, the first thing I would have done was better prepare financially. Secondly, I would have assessed my professional experience to explore how I could leverage my knowledge and skills as an entrepreneur. Like most creative people, I put the cart before the horse. I went through a lot of financial turmoil on my path of entrepreneurship. If you plan accordingly, you can take what you've learned in your place of employment and successfully transition into entrepreneurship without financial turmoil. Here are some creative ways.

Use your professional experience to create an empire. One of my close sister friends, Chelsea Hayes, is successfully building an empire from her professional expertise. She is a natural leader with two bachelor's degrees, one in Public Relations and another in Public Health Promotion, a master's degree in Corporate Communication. Chelsea's education landed her jobs in corporate America with positions focusing on Human Resources. She filled traditional job roles at companies like General Electric, the Los Angeles Sparks, and the

Africa Channel. Chelsea was exposed to entrepreneurship when she helped a friend with a project for the Los Angeles Police Department.

This experience attracted potential clients outside her 9 to 5. Chelsea took what she learned in her traditional job and started the Coaching Factory, where she helps companies and everyday professionals use strategic communications to maximize success. In her full-time job, she focused on the conventional aspects of Human Resources, which usually are hiring and firing. Chelsea took what she learned in corporate America to expand as an entrepreneur. Her clients include General Mills, CBS, and a host of celebrities and high-profile individuals.

Chelsea did not abruptly leave her job to become an entrepreneur. She took strategic steps and built her empire while maintaining employment. After creating a sustainable business, she walked away from corporate America and hasn't looked back. If you are aspiring to be an entrepreneur but currently working a full-time job, start thinking of ways to build on your empire in your current position.

Bring creativity to your current field. The majority of the crowd tends to seek the traditional route of breaking into their industry of choice. They seek the blueprint of other people to see how they can apply it to their professional lives. This is why it can be hard to uncover our purpose. We pursue the conventional route, thinking if success doesn't happen in an orderly fashion, it's not meant for us. If you enter your desired career path using someone else's blueprint, how can you create your own? It's okay to seek inspiration from others but remember this is your journey. God can't perform a miracle in your life if you continue to take the safe route. Like I said before, your God-given talent and abilities have the power to solve some of the world's greatest problems and bring new approaches to old methods.

While working one of my side jobs, I met the CEO of VNG Hoops, Marcus Crenshaw. He is the perfect example of bringing creativity to his current field. He used his experience playing college and professional basketball to help change the world of women's basketball. His love for basketball came at an early age while growing up in Detroit, Michigan. Like the majority of athletes, he had dreams of going to the NBA. Marcus played collegiate basketball at California State Fullerton and earned his Bachelors in African American Studies. From there, he went on to play European Basketball for five years. Playing overseas is not as popular as the NBA, but you can make a lucrative income. Instead of spending all his money and balling out of control, Marcus started a business. He created Hoops Cred, the first marketing agency specifically for WNBA players. As an athlete, Marcus was able to identify an opportunity in the market through the WNBA. It's no secret that people are more supportive of male professional basketball players. However, women are marching to the top in every occupation. With people complaining about the lack of coverage for WNBA players, Marcus created *She Hoops Network on*

Instagram, sharing WNBA highlights. The page built over 100k followers in less than a year. The success led to *She Hoops Network* being sold to *Overtime,* a digital sports network for Generation Z.

Marcus has helped build brands and secured endorsement deals while consulting over 30 WNBA athletes. As a sports agent for female athletes, he uses creative ways to fulfill his clients' needs. Professional sports is not your average corporate job, but most people use traditional methods for entry. Most athletes lose a sense of purpose when their dreams of playing professional sports don't come true. Marcus has used his experience as an athlete and entrepreneur to take a new approach in women's basketball.

Create a plan of action. Before leaving my job, I didn't effectively set up a financial plan to stay afloat while tending to my purpose. All I knew was, I had a dream and was ready to fulfill it. I saved up a little money, but in my mind, I was following God's plan. That's all I needed to move forward. While this is true, even ants store up food in the summer to survive in the winter. If an ant can prepare for its present and future, we can too. My failure to plan financially left me broke faster than I intended. Although I am thankful for all the people who helped me during my financial struggles, I could have done a better job of setting myself up to win financially.

My line sister Candace Hansford who my line sisters and I often joke and refer to as "new money," did a great job of preparing financially before starting her private practice. She is currently the owner of Hansford Legal, specializing in estate administration, probable, litigation, and civil litigation. Candace is passionate when it comes to helping individuals, families, and small businesses.

In the Law profession, most seek a traditional route of making partner at a prestigious firm. Candace knew early on that she wanted to create her own instead of working to appease her colleagues for a climb up the ladder. Before attending Chicago-Kent College of Law, she worked in the financial sector for the Office of the Comptroller of Currency (OCC) and later the Financial Industry Regulatory Authority (FINRA). After joining the Illinois Bar, she managed the Inspector General's office for the Public Building Commission of Chicago, where she investigated allegations of fraud, abuse, waste, and corruption within the public works contracts.

Candace accredits successfully starting her own practice to completing a business plan with a budget and revenue projections. She took a realistic view of the costs of creating a new business and the money she could expect to make. After comparing this with her personal budget, Candace determined how much she needed to save before leaving her place of employment. Candace did not leave her job until it made sense according to her business plan.

Those of you who are ready to dive into the world of entrepreneurship, hold on a little longer to determine if it makes financial sense. Create a financial plan that will help make room for your gift. With an effective method intact, it's easier to deal with the overbearing, micromanaging boss or anything that makes you want to run out the door. You will leave when the time is right.

CREATE A JOB FOR YOURSELF

For my friends who are without a 9-5 and struggling to find one, it may be time to put an end to the vicious cycle of putting your destiny in other people's hands and create some opportunities. When I first began to describe going for yours as creating an opportunity instead of waiting for it, I didn't fully comprehend the significance of this phrase. Honestly, it was just something that had a nice ring to it. I began to understand its depth when I had no other choice but to create an opportunity for myself.

Our current generation is making it more common to create jobs instead of waiting to be hired. I've always admired the way writer/actress Issa Rae opened a door for herself when she created *Awkward Black Girl*, a web-series she premiered on YouTube. A few years later, her show *Insecure* was picked up by HBO. Issa tapped into her own resources by gathering talented friends and developing a show instead of waiting for someone to give her permission. If it weren't for showcasing her work on YouTube, we might not know the beautiful and talented soul we know as Issa Rae.

The same goes for Rapper/Singer/Songwriter, Chancelor Bennett affectionately known as Chance the Rapper. While most aspiring music artists spend time trying to appease record labels and A&R executives hoping to get signed, Chance did the opposite and made music for free. He chose the independent route yet won Best Rap Album at the GRAMMY Awards for *Coloring Book* and many wins and nominations that year. This doesn't just apply to people in entertainment. The obstacles you are facing could be a segway to hiring yourself. There are no limits to what you can create on your own.

Hire Yourself. In the words of one of my favorite rappers Big Sean, "*I made myself a boss, and then I gave me a promotion.*" Being turned down from multiple jobs has turned me into a certified GIRL BOSS. But it didn't come easy. The great thing about it is, I took everything I learned while working a 9-5 and applied it to my own business. I work for myself just as hard (maybe even harder) as I did when I was working a regular 9-5. Treating entrepreneurship as if it were a 9-5 will help you move forward in your professional goals. On a spiritual level, I engage in my work keeping in mind that I have answered the Lord's call. Taking on this attitude will help you execute according to your purpose.

Explore all of your gifts. When you hire yourself, you can freely explore all of your talents. During lunch with my sister-friend Reesha Archibald, I inquired about her story of leaving her 9 to 5 and taking out the time to nurture every one of her gifts. Based upon her current career path, you would never know that Reesha once was a Supply Chain Logistics Manager in corporate America. Her job was to ensure suppliers were building quality products.

Reesha entered this field shortly after receiving her Master's Degree from the HBCU Lincoln University. She used her knowledge and expertise while working for corporations like NBC Universal and Boeing. Although she spent years in corporate America, she nurtured her creative gifts in her spare time. She is a talented singer who has a passion for acting, producing, and directing.

When she left her corporate job in 2015, Reesha didn't rush into another opportunity. Instead, she took on various gigs that would allow her to explore her passion. I would stand amazed as I watched her sing in Kanye's Sunday service choir, work as a Producer at Cedric the Entertainer's production company while working alongside former journalist turned television writer and producer Cheo Hodari Coker as His Executive Assistant.

Of course, I had to find out how she went from being a Supply Chain Logistics Manager to her current business endeavors. Reesha explained to me that although she had a demanding job, she always sought ways to tap into her creative side. Whether it was singing backup at a local event, or acting in a short film, she made a vow to herself that she would never let go of her creative side. Growing up in a home where creativity was encouraged, Reesha enjoyed using her singing and acting skills. Never letting go of her creative side is what helped Reesha make her skills transferable in entertainment. Her job in supply chain logistics provided her with the project management skills to fulfill her current projects. Most recently, she was an Executive Producer on a Dramedy on Bounce TV. Tapping into her creative side while working her 9 to 5 helped open doors when she left Corporate America.

Identify available resources. There are so many resources for entrepreneurs that will help make your business flourish. Now is the perfect time to see what type of assistance is available for you as an entrepreneur. We will discuss further when we get to the *Don't Wait Create Model*. Whether you have a 9-5 with a creative side or looking to be a full-time entrepreneur, there is room for you. As you explore your forever growing purpose, start thinking about how you can tap into your purpose while fulfilling your day-to-day responsibilities. Grab your Don't Wait Create and answer the following questions.

1. After reading this chapter, what's your understanding of a job vs. purpose?
2. Have there been times when you confused your job with your purpose? If so, how?
3. Which type of creator are you? The 9 to 5 with creative on the side? Or a creator with a side gig?
4. How will knowing what type of creator you are, help you with your overall goals?

THE CREATOR'S MINDSET

Look at what God made, I'm God-like, the image of well done,
I'm too nice
—*Make it Easy,* Big K.R.I.T.

W alking away from my full-time job in Chicago felt like one of the most liberating moments in my life. Finally, I would be able to pursue my dream without the hassle of being micromanaged. Leaving my job felt like the answer to all my prayers. For the first time in years, I could sleep in, and prevent maneuvering through the heavy snowfall on my way to work. I could work when I felt like it because now, I created my own schedule. At least that's what I thought.

I can't help but laugh when I think about what I initially imagined going for mine to be. I am thankful my exaggerated thoughts made me focus on all of the possibilities instead of worrying about the obstacles ahead. If I had any idea of the setbacks I would experience, I probably would have never left my job.

Excited about my new life, I called my good friend and brother Malik Yusef to tell him I had finally taken the giant leap. Malik is a Grammy-Award winning writer and has helped write songs for talented artists, including Kanye West, Ty Dolla $ign, and John Legend. He was one of the very first people that taught me the importance of having the right mindset. After I shared my news, he responded, "That's great; I'm about to pick you up."

"What do you mean? There's a snowstorm; I'm not going outside." I was frustrated because all I wanted to do was relax and eventually figure out my next move. I have come to learn that when you are incredibly passionate about something, you will find a way to navigate through the rain, sleet, and snow.

"You're going to need some type of income; I could use an assistant. You can work with me until you finish writing your book; this will also give you a chance to experience the grind on a new level" It didn't sound like a bad idea; after all, I had quit my job, so the odds of me receiving unemployment were slim.

When he arrived, Malik gave me some advice I will never forget. He looked me square in the eye and said, *"If you are serious about Going for Yours, you have to put in work. You have to know the difference between being a dog and a wolf. A dog is comfortable knowing when his next meal is coming. But a wolf goes out to hunt their prey because they know they can only eat what they kill. An entrepreneur has to move in the spirit of the wolf, initiating their next opportunity."*

At my full-time job, I was comfortable. Similar to a house trained dog, I knew when my next paycheck was coming. My salary wasn't huge, but my next check came like clockwork. Not knowing where or when I would receive any type of compensation really scared me. Without a job, I had to take on the spirit of the wolf. However, my mentality was still very much of a dog. A wolf walks in authority because they know what they're capable of achieving. They recognize their strength. Taking on the mindset of a wolf means that you may not know where your next meal or check will come from, but you know the creator will provide for you every step of the way.

At that time, I was receiving advice from someone who was born into an abusive childhood and went from gangbanging to becoming a talented songwriter. Malik is a living example of the advice he had just given me. Anyone who knows him would tell you that he lives in his own world. He marches to the beat of his drum, taking full responsibility for his dream in the spirit of the wolf. It's the mindset and lifestyle he has created. For Malik, there is no idea or vision too big for him to accomplish. Once you believe you can achieve what God has called you to do, you will march to the beat of your drum, knowing that anything is possible.

For the next few months, while writing my book, I assisted Malik with various projects. I watched as he created opportunities for himself that the average person wouldn't dare to explore. There were times Malik would call Kanye to see where he was recording and spend his own money to fly wherever he was so he could help work on an album. He didn't wait on a phone call. He initiated the opportunity and made sure he was in the room with the people who could help take his vision a step further.

One day, while riding to an event, he pulled out a notebook of lyrics he had written. "I wrote a song for Beyoncé," he said confidently.

"Really? Does she like it?"

"She doesn't know about it yet; I have no idea why she would want to use it. I just had her in mind when I wrote it."

"Okay...." I shrugged it off a bit, wondering how he would get a song to Beyoncé. I know he has worked with Kanye, but we were talking about the one and only Queen Bey this time.

At the time of our conversation, I would have never known that a few short years later, some of the lyrics he shared in the car that day, would be heard in *Sandcastles*, a song on Beyoncé's sixth studio album, the infamous *Lemonade*. When I got closer to completing my book, I stopped working with Malik and used all of my time and energy to get to the finish line. But it was just enough time to help me develop a new mindset for the journey ahead. When you are called to create, your level of thinking can bring you closer or further from what God has planned for you. Creating something well beyond your imagination is not for the timid or faint of heart.

THE PATH TO A CREATOR'S MINDSET

When it comes to having a creator's mindset, I can't help but think of the *Go for Yours* logo created by Jeremiah

Myles. People often ask, why is there a car, house, and diamond in the logo? All three symbols represent the material items some people hope to obtain, but there is a deeper meaning behind the symbols. The car is for the drive it takes to make your dreams a reality, the house is an example of the foundation that you must build, and the diamond serves as a reminder that the real power is inside of you. All three are essential when having the mindset of a creator.

CREATING WITH DRIVE

"Grind hard but got a lot to show for it, always had drive like I had to chauffeur it."
—Big Sean, *My Last*

Imagine receiving a phone call letting you know that you've just inherited a million dollars. To claim it, all you have to do is drive to the destination where your inheritance awaits. After being provided with the address, you put it into your GPS. Ten minutes into your drive, it begins to rain. No big deal, you just put on the windshield wipers and keep driving. Five minutes later, you find out your exit is closed due to construction, causing a twenty-minute delay. As you review the signs for the detour, you notice your car is running out of gas. You were so excited about your inheritance that you forgot to stop for gas on the way. Thankfully, you make it just in time before your car stops. Just when you get comfortably back into your vehicle, ready to make it to your destination, you get a flat tire. An hour after roadside assistance arrives, you finally make it to receive your inheritance. Despite all the setbacks, you are still able to collect what is rightfully yours.

I'm sure by now you catch my drift. When you have a goal in mind, quitting is not an option. Your drive is what gets you to the finish line. It takes a passionate person to go the distance and accomplish what they have committed to achieving. Creating opportunities involves having a certain level of ambition, and it begins with a drive. There is an inheritance waiting just for you. It would be best if you were driven enough to move toward it. Like driving a car, get behind the wheel and do whatever it takes to reach your destination.

Create A Foundation:
"I'm putting down my plan like an architect."
—Slum Village, *Climax*

I always enjoy watching the development of a new house. From the ground up, I've witnessed some beautiful homes come to life. Day by day, workers come together and build from the architect's blueprint. But before any framing, plumbing, or insulation is applied, the foundation must be made. The reason behind the foundation is to hold up and hold together the structure above it. A foundation built correctly increases the amount of abuse a house structure can take and remain safe for the people inside it. Without a solid foundation, the house is useless. Before they begin constructing the foundation, the architect needs to excavate and become familiar with the land. Excavation is the removal of something to create space for something new.

The same applies to your dream. In an ideal world, you will come up with an idea and achieve overnight success. It's hard not to think this way when we become aware of successful individuals at the height of their careers. Unless you pay close attention or follow their story, they may trick you into thinking success happens immediately. Every person with an account of success had to create a foundation to become the person they are today. Start working on your foundation and make room for what is about to happen in your life.

Like the architect needs to excavate, think about what you need to do to create space for the new thing ready to come into your life. What habits are you trying to break? Are there any relationships you need to end? Start building your foundation and work to remove anything that is preventing you from moving forward.

Failure to create a solid foundation is the fastest way to fail. You must take vital steps to support your growth and development. There is no way around putting in the time and effort needed to achieve your goals. It may be as simple as developing a product before you begin to promote it. Or practicing before you showcase your talent. However this applies, make sure you build a foundation for your creation to stand on solid ground.

YOU ARE THE TRUE DIAMOND:
"We're beautiful like diamonds in the sky...shine bright like a diamond."
—Rihanna, *Diamonds*

A diamond is the strongest, most precious stone. It is even regarded as a stone of exceptional power as it can reach into us and open many spiritual doors. When creating, always remember that you are a rare jewel that was created for something unique. Because you were made in God's image, you possess the power to carry out every assignment you were destined for. You don't need permission to use it; all you need is God's blessing. Everything you see around you was created by a human being who tapped into their God-given power. Of course, people will help you along the way. But primarily because they are attracted to the light beaming inside of you and want to help bring it out.

In the early stages of following my dream, I didn't realize the strength I had to manifest my heart's desires. I found myself placing value on everything other than myself. When I began to realize I possessed everything I needed, things started to fall into place. Within, I discovered a real diamond. There is a brand-new person inside of you ready to burst.

Creating your masterpiece starts with your mindset. Without the proper state of mind, everything else I share will be useless. The condition of your life is a direct result of your thoughts. Your level of thinking can bring you closer or further from what God has planned for you. In *Go for Yours*, I encourage readers to have a great attitude and positive spirit. As I began to evolve, I learned this is just the beginning. The core of your thinking has to be rooted in the One who created you. It's the very thing that will improve your life.

Everyone that God has called to create will experience a time where their thoughts attack them. As soon as you are ready to begin your creative journey, the enemy will try to fill your mind with lies. If your thoughts are full of worry, depression, and fear, your dreams will seem impossible. Similar to a wolf, you have to move in confidence that you have everything needed to fulfill your goals. Before you step into your calling, evaluate your mindset. Answer the following questions in your journal.

1. Based on the description in this chapter, have I been operating in the mindset of a dog or wolf?
2. How can I create with drive?
3. What do I need to do to build a foundation?
4. In what ways can I better understand that the real diamond is within me?

5

THE FEAR OF CREATING

"I have learned over the years that when one's mind is made up, this diminishes fear; knowing what must be done does away with fear."
— Rosa Parks

According to an article in *Psychology Today*, fear is a basic human emotion wired into our systems for a beneficial purpose—to signal us in times of danger and prepare us physically to accomplish what is necessary for survival. What was initially created to prevent us from harm, has turned into a mechanism that produces barriers to all the great things we can achieve. My decision to wait stemmed from the monogamous relationship I had with fear. Like many unhealthy relationships, it's what delayed me from fully walking in my purpose. Fear did everything in its power to stop me from embracing what would ultimately change the direction of my life. The on and off relationship had me questioning my self-worth and ability to accomplish something that was already written in the stars for me to achieve.

Having a creator's mindset doesn't always come easy. Fear is one of the biggest obstacles you will have to overcome. It's impossible to make sound decisions if you are operating in fear. Choices that stem from anxiety is the fastest way to sabotage all of the blessings readily available for you. Any thought or emotion opposite of a sound mind does not come from God. They are the result of thinking in the natural. No matter your level of faith, fear will always try to show itself mighty. Let's take some time to explore some fears that may be causing you to wait instead of create.

FEAR OF THE UNKNOWN

As it relates to writing my books, I vowed to be as open and transparent as humanly possible. I am committed to sharing stories that will help change the narrative for people who have been afraid to step out on faith. Talking about my fears breeds a sense of vulnerability, making it one of the most candid sections you will read. To be completely honest, nothing has brought me more anxiety than fear of the unknown. It's one thing to wonder what will happen in the next episode of *Power*, but when it comes to my life, that's another story. The older I get, the more this fear tries to come and knock me off of my game.

I was most fearful of creating because I had a plan mapped out of what I thought my life should be. Because I didn't know where my passion would take me, I stayed at my traditional job longer than I needed to. I wasn't delighted, but I knew money would be deposited in my account on the first and fifteenth. If I quit, how would I pay my bills? How will I get out of my grandmother's basement? What if this was just a silly dream leading me to a dead-end? I had no idea where this journey would take me, and sometimes it drove me crazy trying to figure it out.

The biggest fears came from the idea of putting my personal goals on hold, leaving me with more what-ifs. What if I'm lonely for the rest of my life because I spent my entire youth following my dream? What if I can't have babies because I waited too long? What if I never meet someone who truly understands my calling? What if my family stops supporting my dream? These were all fears that almost made me stick to living a life that appeared to be safe, rather than take the unpredictable route.

It's normal to want all the details before you begin a new adventure. But no matter how much you plan, there will be some things you can't control. You will never have the full picture of what God is trying to do in your life. Isaiah 55:8-9 tells us, "*for my thoughts are higher than your thoughts, neither are your ways my ways....as the heavens are higher than the earth, so are my ways higher than your ways and my thoughts higher than your thoughts.*" God's thoughts are higher than our thoughts, and His ways are higher than our ways. When you get caught up in worrying about your future, remember that God knows every detail. Because His thoughts are higher than ours, we will not fully comprehend everything He is doing at the exact moment it's happening. It's essential to have the patience to see how things unfold.

One of the most rewarding opportunities that opened up during my journey of creating was teaching part-time at a performing arts college. During my critical thinking class, I assigned students to write a paper that described their life's philosophy. Savannah, a student, majoring in dance, shared her perspective of the unknown. Instead of being afraid, she viewed the unknown as a blank canvas waiting for a beautiful picture to be painted. As she shared her point of view, it's like a light bulb went off. Why haven't I looked at the unknown as the beautiful story God is creating? Savannah's perspective on the unknown made me more excited about my future.

As I reflect on all the great things that happened during my journey, most weren't planned. Everything that came unexpectedly turned out better than I had imagined. These unexpected experiences are the beautiful canvas Savannah was referring to. Life will bring some of the most unpredictable surprises. Both good and bad. When the challenges come, you will discover a more robust version of yourself. Since your dream is rooted in purpose, God will give you the knowledge and strength to overcome every unknown obstacle. It's time to get excited about the unknown with confidence that a beautiful picture is being created on your blank canvas. I can't begin to fathom all the things that are in store for you. Whatever you encounter, please be sure to share your testimony with me.

FEAR OF REJECTION

In the spirit of being forthright, I have no other choice but to tell you that the fear of rejection has haunted me since the fifth grade. Maybe even earlier than that. I feared being rejected by my friends, teachers, and even the guys I liked for over twenty years. There were a host of opportunities I did not pursue in fear of being rejected. Even when I did go after something I wanted, I didn't give it my all. My deep fear of rejection had created a wall that prevented me from giving 100% in any endeavor I pursued. This showed in my grades, performance in sports, and in my personal relationships. I have made some of the most immature decisions that stemmed from my fear of rejection.

As I reminisce, this fear probably came at such an early age because I grew up in a predominantly white town with very little diversity. Although I had black friends, we were usually placed in different classes, leaving us to be the only person of color in our class. I can recall being rejected by teachers who didn't see my full potential, therefore, not encouraging me to do my best. The fear of rejection is one of the strongest fears people have to overcome because, for most of us, it was established in our childhood and followed us into adulthood. This fear speaks to the child in us that was rejected by our parents, peers, or authoritative figures. Its power has led many people to extreme insecurity and self-doubt and is potent enough to diminish any dream before you get started.

If you are afraid of rejection, you are not alone. But to be quite frank, there is no way around being rejected. On the bright side, we can change the way we view rejection. Starting with knowing that rejection is God's protection and redirection. I can't begin to explain the joy I feel when I think about how the rejection I faced was protecting and realigning me with my purpose. I won't go into detail just yet. However, I am thankful for disappointments that came in the form of rejection. Overcoming the fear of rejection requires knowing that what's meant for you will never pass you. As hard as it was to experience, it enhanced my creativity, helped me grow, and led me to new opportunities.

.

Fear Of Failure

Most people (myself included) want to be like the DJ Khaled song and *"win, win, win, no matter what!"* By human nature, we focus so much on winning and forget that failure is part of the journey. The fear of failure is what makes some of us quit before we even start. If it's not enough to make us stop, we begin to make safe and predictable decisions. This fear is what keeps us in our comfort zone and living a life filled with the same routine.

Fear of failing an exam, being fired from work, or bombing an interview, the list goes on. Depending on the severity, the fear of failure can cause stress and anxiety that will wake you up in the middle of the night with a panic attack. Similar to rejection, there is no way around failing. The great thing is, failure will help shape your success. In most cases, you are creating a blueprint as you go. So, you are bound to make mistakes. As you are being stretched and molded, a majority of your lessons will come from failure. Failing does not diminish the calling on your life. It strengthens it.

One of the best ways to overcome fear is to change your attitude about failure. In my professional career, I have taken on many projects filled with multiple moving parts. In some instances, my advancement depended on how well I executed each project. The fear of failure is what drove me to the finish line. What has helped me the most is thinking about the worst that could happen and being comfortable with every potential outcome, even the possibility of failure. Remembering that in the end, I will end up exactly where I was meant to be. As you read further, I will provide you with some examples of how I failed forward by turning my obstacles into opportunities.

We've all heard it before; you miss 100% of the shots you don't take. Don't miss out on something because you are afraid to fail. You will win some and lose some, and that's just the nature of the game. Failure does not diminish who God has created you to be. From Steve

Jobs to Warren Buffet, every successful person has experienced an extreme loss. Some of your losses will be more extreme than others. But they will make for a better story.

FEAR OF WHAT OTHERS THINK

I took longer than I should have to answer my calling in fear of what others would think. I was 27 years old when I came up with the concept for *Go for Yours*. I don't know what it is, but there was something about my late twenties that made me feel like I needed to accomplish everything before my 30th birthday. Not even taking into consideration that there is a whole life beyond thirty. I was hesitant because I didn't want this dream to cause me to live in my grandmother's basement beyond my thirtieth birthday, which it did. But it wasn't so bad after all.

I can't help but think about how silly my thoughts were. I didn't realize the blessing of living with my grandmother when a lot of people wish their grandparents were still around. Instead, I focused on what everyone else thought I should be doing. To have someone like my grandmother believe in my dream when she came from a completely different generation is a big deal. Although she didn't understand the entire vision, she supported it. There were times when I overheard her on the phone explaining to her friends what I was working on. Although she supported me, some people felt I needed a "real" job. I even had people take digs at my personal life. Overhearing other family members share the importance of being married early or assuming that I would rather work the rest of my life than raise a family of my own.

Once you decide to go against the grain, people will be waiting to share their opinion about you. It's just one of the many sacrifices you make when deciding to pursue something most people wouldn't dare to. There will always be someone who wants to give their two cents about what you should be doing, how you should be doing it, and when. It takes a strong person to walk in their God-given purpose. As soon as you take the first step, you will approach someone trying to project their opinions on you.

If they aren't telling you to your face, they give their opinion about you to someone else. Honestly, their opinion of you isn't even your business. Another person's limited view should not negatively impact what you have going on. I have chosen to ignore the opinions of people who think they know how I should be living my life. I encourage you to do the same. Worrying about what others think will drown out the inner voice telling you to step into your purpose.

I have also learned to be mindful of who I talk about my dreams to. I remember sharing my dream of being a news reporter with some of my classmates in high school. Clear as day, I recall us being in foods class where I told them that being a news anchor would be pretty cool. One replied, *"that would never happen."* I don't think she was diminishing my capabilities. Well, maybe she was. I would like to believe her vision was limited.

Living in a small town like DeKalb, Illinois, she probably couldn't figure out how a black girl from a small town could make such a dream come true. This thought was diminished immediately, and I never thought about being a news reporter again. But guess what happened? A black girl who grew up in the same small town and graduated a few years after me made this impossible dream come true in her life. Her name is Janai Norman, and you can find her on Good Morning America. Don't ever let anyone's opinion stop you from doing what you are destined to do. Protect your dream and be mindful of what you share.

It's time to address the fears holding you back. When we do, you will come to find that the chances of them actually happening are slim to none. Don't allow an imaginary failure to stop you from moving forward. Most of the things you fear will never come to pass. It's just the enemy's tactic to scare you away from your dreams. There is not one fear that is powerful enough to stop you from your purpose unless you let it. If you have put your goals on hold because of fear, it's time to address them. Below are a few signs that will help determine if you are letting fear get in the way.

1. You have stopped or delayed pursuing your passion to avoid being rejected or hearing the word "no."
2. The fear of failure stops you in your tracks.
3. You make calculated decisions instead of taking risks that can lead to a better life.
4. You decide to settle for what you already

have because you don't feel like the life you imagine is for you.

5. The possibility of failure trumps the likelihood of succeeding.
6. You avoid anything new or unknown.
7. You procrastinate.
8. Receiving approval from others is important to you.
9. You try to control everything.

In your Don't Wait Create journal, write down which fear you relate to the most. Why do you think you have this fear? What are some ways you can overcome this fear? Is there any fear you are trying to overcome not mentioned in the list of fears

It can be challenging to move forward in your destiny with common fears tugging at you. In your journal, write down every fear that you have. Next, I want you to replace it with the truth. Here's an example:

Fear: I fear that if I start a new business, I will fail.

Truth: A new business comes with its share of obstacles, and I will work through any failure that I may experience.

Fear: I fear that if I drop the ball on this project, my supervisor will fire me.

Truth: A job doesn't determine my destiny; I can always get another one.

. . .

The purpose of this activity is to address your fears and replace them with the truth and move in the direction of your dreams with confidence. After this activity, write down which fear you relate to the most. Where does it stem from? What are some ways you can overcome this fear?

6

CREATE YOUR DEFINITION OF SUCCESS

"So how does it feel to be successful?" A young lady inquired from me while speaking to a group of students where I attended graduate school. *Go for Yours* had become a required text in the Black Studies Program, and standing before me was a group of young, bright-eyed undergrads viewing me as an example of success. To them, I was successful because I was a published author who had multiple celebs holding up my book in random pics on my Instagram page. Unbeknownst to them, I hadn't viewed myself as successful. Although it seemed like I was making strides, it took work to get those photo ops, and I was still living in my grandmother's basement. I felt I hadn't reached my vision of success.

To go along with their perception, I replied with an embellished description of what it felt like to be successful. I shared my story of having the best life ever because I chose to "go for mine." As they looked to me for guidance, I encouraged each one of them to follow their dreams. My presentation went well, and of course, I provided the class with some tools that would help them reach their goals. But it could have been so much more powerful if I had the guts to tell them of the setbacks I had experienced. Reminiscing on this moment makes me wish I could go back in time and be more transparent about what it's really like to pursue your dream. There were times when I was struggling financially to keep up. I would be overcome with anxiety because I was worried about failing at work. Furthermore, I had other goals I wanted to accomplish, and they seemed so far away.

Looking back, I can genuinely say I was successful. It was hard for me to see because I was comparing it to others. I had successfully published a book that was being used as a curriculum, was being booked for multiple speaking engagements around the city, and even did a couple of grade school commencement speeches. I was surrounded by people who loved me and believed in my dream; I still had a roof over my head, a car to drive, and did not miss a meal. The things I was hoping to achieve were headed in my direction. I just didn't realize it at that moment. Being caught up in what I thought following my dream should look like made me minimize all the great things happening around me.

Thankfully, over the years, my idea of success has evolved. Living in a world where people will try to sell the illusion of success has forced me to define success on my terms. Instead of describing it in a shallow way, I view success as the ability to wholeheartedly follow my dream while being financially stable, healthy (emotionally and physically), and enjoying life with my family and friends. Now, when I stand in front of an audience who wants to know how it feels to be successful, I can answer with complete honesty and transparency. But not before inquiring what success looks like for them. Having the wrong idea is the fastest way to steer your dream in a direction it is not meant to be. Before you begin defining what success looks like for you, let's talk about what it's not.

ACCOLADES DO NOT EQUAL SUCCESS

After asking my critical thinking class to share their idea of success, one of my students, Charles, shared his goal of winning a Tony Award. As a talented performer, he wants to be recognized in Broadway Theatre. I believe this is possible for him and wanted to assure Charles that he can still have a successful career whether or not he receives any accolades. The same applies to you.

It is common to want to receive recognition for your work. In fact, it is a dream of mine to receive a Pulitzer Prize or an NAACP Image Award. But if I never make the *New York Times Best-Seller* list or receive any of the prestigious accolades that were created by the hands of man, I am happy knowing I followed what God put in my heart to do. That's greater than any accolade I could ever earn. If you never receive the acknowledgment you think you deserve, it does not diminish your value as a person. You were made in the image of God. What better award could you ask for?

Do not dedicate all your hard work and energy just for the sake of acknowledgment. It's a great feeling to be recognized, but it does not determine your worth. J. Cole, another one of my favorite rappers in this generation, once shared in a tweet, *"I went through a lot of heartbreak the first half of my career, maybe even longer, cuz deep down I needed that validation that I thought the awards could bring."* He is a talented rapper, producer, and songwriter whose music has touched millions of people, including myself. Yet, he almost got caught up in putting his validation in awards and accolades. I had the honor of meeting and having a conversation with J. Cole after one of his concerts.

After writing *Go for Yours*, I always had a copy with me. Before the concert started, I gave a copy to the promoter to give to J. Cole. To my surprise, he wanted to meet the person who gifted him with the book. After the concert, I was escorted to the green room, where he was talking to his friends and fans. He stepped outside, and we talked for about ten minutes. I will never forget how shocked I was when he told me he feels like we met before. I reminded him that we had met about a year earlier at an event in Los Angeles.

To have a strong sense of humility after you have sold millions of records, now that's success. No plaque can compare to the people that have been touched by his music. I feel the same way when someone tells me how much reading one of my books or hearing my story has touched them. You should not measure your success based upon accolades but instead, the people you will impact because you answered God's call, even if it's just one person. It's fun to be recognized, but your gift was created for a much deeper purpose. Your journey will more than likely lead to moments of being celebrated. Just make sure it's not the main reason you are following your dream.

Money Does Not Equal Success

I grew up in the era where gator boots and a pimped out Gucci suit meant success for many people. It didn't matter how much money they had in their bank account as long as there was enough to drive the latest car and rock the flyest gear. I'm sure my Big Tymers reference probably dated myself, but nonetheless, money plays a huge role when it comes to people's perception of success.

Social media gurus and self-made millionaires often encourage people to seek million-dollar success. There is nothing wrong with being wealthy, but the amount of money you make is not the determining factor of your success. As someone who has answered what God is calling them to do, I always keep Matthew 16:26 in mind. *"For what profits a man if he gains the whole world but loses his own soul?"* The collection of possessions can bring out the worst in some people. I know that won't be you. Also, remember money doesn't determine happiness. I have witnessed millionaires who are clinically depressed and broke people who are extremely happy. Although money is a necessary aspect of life, it is not a measurement of how successful you are. It's crucial to understand this concept, so you don't get caught up in chasing your dreams for the sole purpose of being rich. Going for yours while staying connected to the essence of who you are is something money can't buy.

Instead of focusing on wanting to be rich, start working on goals that lead to financial stability. When creating an opportunity, a lot of your financial resources will be tied up into your dream. It can be tough to focus on your goals while worrying about how you will keep the lights on. Pursuing your dream to become a millionaire can add a new level of stress, and that will give you a false sense of progress.

When I decided to work on the Go for Yours Foundation full-time while living in Los Angeles, I experienced a lot of financial stress. While having dinner with my friend Taylor, she gave me some sound advice that helped me with my financial woes. *"You have to think about how much it costs to be you and figure out how you can generate income,"* she told me. "*Once you determine your number, anything extra is a bonus."* Together, we came up with creative ways to help me stay afloat while building my enterprise. Her piece of advice has made my life less stressful. Focus on building financial stability and identify ways to grow your money instead of focusing solely on being rich.

If you are considering being self-employed, I suggest creating a financial plan that will help you stay afloat. No matter how positive you are, worrying about money can take a toll on you mentally and physically. Instead of chasing a dream to become rich, start thinking about how much income you need to live as an entrepreneur. Become knowledgeable on how you can invest, grow, and leave a legacy behind.

FAME DOES NOT MEAN SUCCESS

"I want to be famous," a student told me at a high school I was speaking at. She shared her desire to be extremely famous to the point she couldn't leave the house without being stopped by the paparazzi. This young lady is just one of many people I have met and want to achieve goals that lead to fame. Living my dream has led me down a path of meeting and knowing famous people. It always amazes me when people tell me they are proud of me after seeing me post a picture with one of my well-known friends. I get more engagement from posting a celebrity than any other post. We live in a world where people glorify being rich and famous. Instead of creating quality content, people are often more focused on getting likes and views. Many folks are well-known for various reasons and can't even afford to pay their bills. So does a million views or paparazzi outside your window really mean you are successful?

There is nothing wrong with being well-known but chasing a dream for the sake of being famous is not something you should strive for. It's just another way to put your destiny in other people's hands. As shared in the first edition of *Go for Yours*, success can be seen behind the scenes. The most significant people in the world are the ones you will never know or meet. It's the people behind the scenes who make famous people so important and successful. Most people who achieve and maintain fame have a powerful team behind them.

If you were to ask a famous person about their experiences with fame, I'm sure they would tell you that it's overrated. For starters, so many folks want your time and money. You are not always sure who you can trust because people want to be around you for the wrong reasons. If that's not enough, you can barely walk through a crowded room without being stopped multiple times. People stay in your business, and it's even hard to eat at a restaurant without someone wanting a photo op. Most of all, fame is fleeting. If you do something against popular opinion, people are quick to "cancel" you. If you aren't frequently in the media, people view you as irrelevant. Pursue your dreams because it's something you are passionate about, not because you are seeking fame.

If you become well-known, it will be for all the right reasons.

Success Is More Than Talent

If all we needed were talent, doors would be swinging open for everybody. It takes more than talent to thrive in your purpose. What's your work ethic? Do you follow through on your word? Are you a pleasure to be around? These qualities go beyond talent.

In my eagerness to publish *Go for Yours,* I skipped over

key steps that were fundamental to my success. I failed to create a plan to market and sell my book. I thought all I needed was my project. I hadn't even set a goal of how many copies I wanted to sell. One person we can all learn from is comedian turned mogul Kevin Hart. In a world with thousands of people pursuing a similar dream, he has implemented an impeccable marketing strategy, built a reliable team, and continues to work hard. In the first edition of *Go for Yours*, I shared a story about how I watched Kevin's career flourish before my eyes. His story is one that inspired me to look into the lives of others and share their journey of success. The first time I met Kevin, he was by himself at an after-party at Illinois State University, where I attended as an undergrad. He was standing by himself, and anyone could walk up to him and say "hello." The third time I met him, I was standing in a long line at Walmart waiting to get my DVD signed and, of course, give him a copy of Go *for Yours*.

After we took our picture and Kevin signed my DVD, I told him about *Go for Yours* and gave him an autographed copy. His initial reaction was to take another picture holding the book. His exact words, *"you need this for marketing purposes."* We took our second picture with both of us holding the book. My picture with Kevin is one of my favorite celebrity photos in the *Go for Yours* archives.

Kevin has brought new strategies to a career that people have been pursuing for years. The world has no choice but to know who he is because he is continuously starring in new films, traveling the world on tour, and launching 5K morning runs with his fans around the country. His success goes way beyond having talent. Take a step back and think about what you can do outside your talent to thrive in your gift. You can be the most talented person in the world, but you might as well quit while you're ahead if you lack in other areas. You will have to create strategies to put you ahead of the game.

If you don't define success on your terms, someone else will define it for you. It's up to you to determine what it means to live your best life. You know what time it is. Grab your journal and take some time to think about what success looks like for you. Be as descriptive as possible without leaving one single detail as you write your vision of success.

If you are stuck on how to begin the process of imagining your success, I recommend doing what Steve Harvey advised audience members on his talk show. You can also find this piece of advice on YouTube. Steve tells them to write down everything they want to accomplish. He advises them to think of 300 things they would like to accomplish. It may sound like a lot for most, but the purpose of this number is to help people open up their imagination because most of us are conditioned to think on a small scale.

When you have a clear vision of what success means to you, it's easier to create a plan to achieve your goals. It also reduces the anxiety that comes with the illusion of success. As you grow, your idea of success will more than likely change, but at least you have something to refer to when others attempt to define success for you.

7

CREATE OPPORTUNITIES OUT OF OBSTACLES

"If I ever took a loss, it was a lesson."
—Lecrae, *Blessings*

On the outside looking in, 2013 was an excellent year for me. I was a published author, speaker, and budding entrepreneur. I was going for mine, but I was broke. Not just any kind of broke; I could barely pay for my cell phone. Parking tickets with a boot on my car broke. Borrowing your best friend's clothes for a speaking engagement broke. I was experiencing one of the most uncomfortable seasons of my life. To be quite frank, I didn't want to be a wolf anymore. It was time for another plan.

The beginning stages of *Go for Yours* was filled with enthusiasm that made it feel like a new relationship. You know, the type where you can't stop thinking about that particular person all day? You find ways to bring them up in conversations and reasons to send a text or phone call. This was the feeling I had while discovering my new gift. It brought on a new level of happiness that made me forget about any obstacles headed in my direction. My fascination with my dream is what gave me the confidence to leave my full-time job and live in my grandmother's basement a little longer. The original plan was to publish *Go for Yours and* make a career out of selling books and speaking engagements. In my mind, I had created something extraordinary, and it wouldn't be hard to thrive. I sold a nice amount of copies and booked some speaking engagements, but it was not enough to support me financially.

Similar to a relationship, my infatuation stage was coming to an end. It was time to make some moves. I was caught between wanting to follow through on my dream and knowing when I would receive my next check. I decided to go back to what was familiar and began to apply for jobs. I landed a variety of interviews for positions with impressive salaries and benefits. When it came to making a decision to hire, I was often told I was a great candidate, but they decided to go with someone else, hire internally, or put the hiring process on hold. Not being able to land a job left me unsure about what was in store for my future.

After spending a gloomy afternoon depressed and trying to figure out my next move, I called one of my good friends and former colleagues, Latrina Fisher. It's so important to talk to people who can see your vision even further than you. Talking to her is what prompted me to turn my obstacles into an opportunity. Latrina asked me, *"Why are you looking for a job? You have something special with Go for Yours. You should create your own program."* I had thought about it before, but it took this moment to remind me that I had the power to create a lane for myself.

It was time for me to model everything I had written about in *Go for Yours*. I immediately stepped out of my discouragement and began expanding on my idea of the Go for Yours Leadership Program, an eight-week curriculum for at-risk youth. The following week, I took a proposal to Julian High School on the south side of Chicago. I chose this school to honor my cousin Ben "Tre" Gibson, who died in 2006 and graduated from the school.

A couple of days after my conversation, I scheduled a meeting with one of the administrators, Mrs. Donna Gentry. She helped me select ten students to pilot the program. While creating a new career path for myself, I didn't even grasp that I was beginning to develop a pathway for young people to follow.

A huge lesson I learned during this time in my life is that I don't determine how long my process will be. Most dreams come with a microwave vision, but it can take years for everything to come full circle. Every dreamer has a journey, and you must understand this if you want to stay the course. Your most significant opportunities will come from overcoming obstacles.

Each stumbling block has created the opportunity for me to improve, strategize, and open a new door resulting in an overall win. My setbacks have been just as powerful as the opportunities I have been blessed to receive. The challenges I faced made me more confident to operate in my gift. They are also what allowed me to experience God's eternal power. With each obstacle was an opportunity to improve, strategize, open a new door, and most importantly, invest in me. In this chapter, I will provide you with some ways to move through your obstacles effectively.

THE OPPORTUNITY TO IMPROVE

When some of our favorite athletes finish a game, they watch the footage to identify opportunities to improve and step up their game. The best way to improve is to reflect on your mistakes and identify opportunities for growth. The various obstacles I faced allowed me to seek ways to improve. I began to reflect on why I was not landing any jobs. Through self-evaluation, I discovered that I was more excited about the salary than the potential jobs. They didn't match my level of experience, drive, or creativity. This was probably apparent in my interviews.

Taking all of this into consideration, I decided only to seek opportunities aligned with my business and brand. When I pitched my program to various schools, I walked into rooms dedicated, knowing I had developed something that would make a massive impact on young people's lives. My passion was so evident that I was offered a part-time job at Julian High School in addition to facilitating my program.

A loss is a perfect opportunity to cultivate your skills, become more polished in your work, and be fully prepared for what's headed in your direction. You will meet various obstacles during your journey. They aren't a reason to give up. Instead, think of ways you can improve. If you are currently experiencing a setback, start exploring ways to enhance your gift.

THE OPPORTUNITY TO STRATEGIZE

Setbacks are also an excellent opportunity to strategize. This gift alone is what has opened many doors for me. I have been able to break down some of the most complex ideas and implement a strategy to put them into practice. A skill I wouldn't have if I hadn't approached obstacles along the way.

It's nearly impossible to dodge closed doors. They will shut right in your face. Some of them are permanent, but a lot of times, they are an opportunity to go back to the drawing board and develop a strategy to see the results you are expecting. It could be as simple as talking to a different person who understands your vision or as complex as creating a new approach to get the results you need to move forward.

Personally, being told "no" by multiple employers led me to strategize a plan of action that helped my dream grow. I decided only to create opportunities that made sense for *Go for Yours* as I developed strategies to strengthen my brand. I began to reach out to more schools, organizations, and churches that would allow me to share my message. I also volunteered in the community and met various people who wanted to support my vision.

For some obstacles, you may be able to prepare ahead. But for the most part, you will need to create new strategies whenever you experience a setback. To better equip yourself, I would recommend writing a business plan, marketing plan, or strategic plan. Even if you do not want to start your own business, you can still create a strategic plan for your professional career. Having your goals outlined will help you strategize as you continue to move forward.

THE OPPORTUNITY TO OPEN A NEW DOOR

Closed doors are the perfect opportunity to enter an open one. One of those doors opened after experiencing so many closed doors was when I signed up to volunteer for Gen 44, a group of millennials in support of President Barack Obama. Without realizing it, I was being rerouted to a path that exceeded my expectations, and my life would soon take a drastic turn. While helping during the reelection campaign, I met so many like-minded, progressive people in the community ready to make a change. One of them being Hollywood actor and author Hill Harper.

During the 2012 election campaign, he traveled to Chicago with President Obama to host a fundraiser. I had been wanting to connect with him because of his passion for empowering the youth. As fate would have it, my best friend Niesha and I were the only volunteers asked to be in charge of check-in for the VIP section. At the close of the event, I introduced myself to him and shared my passion for working with young people. He gave me the contact information for his nonprofit foundation. A few months later, I flew from Chicago to Los Angeles to volunteer as a mentor for the foundation's summer program.

Since I wasn't working at the high school due to the students being on summer vacation, my family helped pay for my flight as a birthday gift. I didn't know anyone who lived in Los Angeles, so my cousin Aundrea arranged for me to stay with her mother-in-law, who resided in Covina. Anyone who lives in Los Angeles knows that it can take up to two hours to get to the city from Covina during heavy traffic hours. For a week, I drove an hour and a half each way to serve as a mentor. That trip was life-changing for me. Not only was I able to volunteer and work with young people, but I also met so many like-minded people walking in their purpose.

I will never forget this period of my life. When I returned from my trip, I had a letter waiting for me from First Lady Michelle Obama. I had given her a book through the secret service during a fundraiser where I served as a volunteer. In her letter, she stated, *each of us can draw inspiration from stories of courage, strength, and perseverance.* This letter was a reminder for me to persevere no matter the obstacle that would come my way.

2012 had its share of closed doors as well as disappointments. About a week after I returned from LA, I lost another cousin to senseless violence, making him the second cousin who did not make it to live past 23. This devastating news made me continue to open doors for myself and others coming behind me. Unfortunately, losing a family member due to senseless violence is a common theme in the African American community. Having two cousins die at such a young age made me want to stay committed to the work I had set forward to do.

The following summer, I was asked to volunteer again with the foundation in LA. This time, I asked to facilitate a *Go for Yours* workshop. The thought of presenting in Los Angeles gave me so much excitement. My brand continued to grow, and I could add to my resume that I presented at this prestigious nonprofit foundation.

On the day of my workshop, I made it my business to put my best foot forward. It's so crazy because I still remember what I was wearing that day. With my black and white shirt, red skirt, and black heels, I gave one of the best presentations of my life. The Executive Director, Akello Stone (Kell) was so impressed with my workshop that he asked if I'd be interested in working with the foundation. They had an opening for an Assistant Director, and he thought I would be perfect for the role. Of course, I would have to get the founder's final approval, but I was supernaturally being led to a door that I didn't attempt to open.

OPPORTUNITY TO REDIRECT YOUR PATH

"We can't afford to hire you, but we are going to invest in you." I was on the phone with Hill, who had just officially

offered me the Assistant Director position. After three years of investing my time, energy, and money into my dream, I had finally made it out of my grandmother's basement in Chicago and was heading to a new life in Los Angeles. Palm trees and Kimora Lee, here I come! The closed doors redirected me to something well beyond my imagination.

Not only is rejection God's protection, but it's redirection. As a creator, I have learned to surrender to God's perfect will for my life. No matter how much I plan, I always make room for God's most pleasant surprises, obstacles, and detours. When you experience barriers, rejection, and defeat, I want to encourage you to stay on the path. Your blessing could be around the corner. What obstacles are you currently facing that you can turn into an opportunity to improve, strategize, or open a new door? Record them in your journal.

8

CREATE, CULTIVATE, AND ELEVATE

"Genius is 1% talent and 99% hard work."
—Albert Einstein

CULTIVATE
Verb (used with object)
To promote or improve growth by labor and attention.

ELEVATE
Verb (used with object)
To move or raise to a higher place or position; lift up.

I eagerly arrived in Los Angeles on a late Friday night, the last day of February in 2014. My first experience with Lyft consisted of the driver picking me up, dropping me off, taking my bags out of the trunk, throwing them in the middle of the street, and speeding off, leaving me in the dust. I was too excited to pay attention to the fact that this man didn't have the common courtesy to make sure I had all my items. I wasn't fazed one bit. I was ready to live my life in the fab lane.

My hard work had finally paid off, and it was time to celebrate the new door that was created just for me. My sister Tiffany flew in the next day to help me settle in. We spent time exploring the city and talked about all the experiences my new life in LA would bring. I was looking forward to frequenting the beach just a few blocks away from my new apartment.

An enthusiastic and very stylish Erika showed up to my role as Assistant Director Monday morning. When I walked into the office, my mouth dropped. It was located in a loft on Hollywood and Vine. The decor was beautiful, and my new boss had all his awards and plaques hanging in a glass case. There was a bookshelf full of books he had published. I felt motivated and grateful that I had been chosen for this position. I didn't take it for granted that there were people who would have loved this position and some who were probably more qualified. I made it known that the foundation would not regret investing in me.

There was a team of five people that handled various entities of Hill's business and brand. Akello and I were in charge of the foundation. He was one of the most energetic people I had ever worked alongside. We were both passionate about making an impact in the lives of the youth we served. We brainstormed during our office meetings, and guess what? Some of our meetings were outside at a Hollywood restaurant, just as I envisioned that snowy day in Chicago.

The culture of the office was relaxed but productive. There were days where I would look out of my office window and see celebrities like Kate Winslet and Stevie Wonder receiving their Hollywood star. This trumped my view in the small office I was used to just a few years earlier. Six weeks into my position, the honeymoon ended. Kell accepted another opportunity, and I had to step up in his role.

As the only person working for the foundation full-time, I was responsible for the summer program, a red-carpet holiday event, and a fundraiser in Washington, DC, in less than twelve months. I was learning the ins and outs of my new job but gladly stepped in as the Interim Executive Director, hoping that this position would become permanent. I quickly learned that my grind was far from over. It had just started.

Cultivating

When creating opportunities to live out your dream, there are levels to this. After the first level of identifying the open doors ready and available to you comes the second level of keeping them open. People often make the mistake of viewing new opportunities as a place of arrival when it's just the beginning. Maintaining this position required me to cultivate and nurture my gifts. How I handled my role as Interim Executive Director would determine the outcome of this opened door. I wasn't going to let any obstacle stand in the way of what was on the other end. As I shared earlier, the foundation couldn't afford to hire me; they just believed in me. If I bombed my trial run, I could have been sent back to Chicago on the first plane smoking.

I was fearful, but I thought of the worst-case scenario and kept pushing for the best, knowing that I would end up exactly where God wanted me to be. I developed a plan and utilized every resource available. The first successful event was the summer program. With the help of our part-time Program Coordinator, volunteers, and friends, we hosted over thirty incoming high school students. I felt relieved.

Next up, the fundraiser in DC. As I juggled my tasks, there was no time to enjoy LA. I was also becoming homesick. Planning a fundraiser that would take place in Washington, DC, while living in Los Angeles was no easy task. I was starting to wonder what I had gotten myself into. Had I bitten off more than I could chew? Not realizing that it was the very thing I needed to prepare me for handling large projects and tasks. The event was similar to Dancing with the Stars. I had to recruit influencers in Washington, DC, to compete and raise money for the foundation. All of the moving pieces almost drive me insane. There was a lot at stake. Thankfully, I hired an event planner and found some dance instructors to teach their partners a routine. Gizelle Bryant, who is now on Housewives of Potomac, was one of the competitors and helped a lot with this event's success, along with Melissa Dawn Simkins. Melissa competed and helped the foundation land corporate sponsors. By the grace of God, we raised over $60,000 for the foundation, and I still had a job.

Next up, the toy drive. This event wasn't as hard because it was one of the most anticipated holiday events in Black Hollywood. 2014 was a year of learning, stretching, and growing. There were times when I would call home crying because I didn't know how I would make it in the position. But what I learned was, sometimes you have to go through the fire to come out shining like a diamond.

ELEVATION

As I said before, there are levels to this. I encourage you to stay the course. Hold your head up and don't give up no matter what. Even if you fail, get back up. 2014 taught me the importance of cultivating my gifts and working to keep the doors open. The success of the events didn't make it any easier. I still had to show myself capable of being the official Executive Director. I mapped out a plan to bring the foundation's programs to Washington, DC, and Baltimore, Maryland. With so many DC natives helping raise money for the foundation, it only seemed right. Helping the foundation go national didn't just elevate my work. It elevated the foundation. We were able to help young people from coast to coast. That was an exciting thing for me. By the end of 2015, I was the Executive Director of the foundation. No more interim.

Who would have imagined all of this happening just

because I decided to volunteer one summer in 2012? I had my share of challenges, but I witnessed what can happen when you are determined to keep your doors open. This is why I am so passionate about making sure you go for yours.

The elevation in my life didn't stop with the foundation. Others became aware of my work with the foundation, and I began consulting people on various projects. Some of the most well respected and admired individuals were wanting to work with me. I was finally starting to enjoy the fruits of my labor. I was enjoying my life, career, and the person I was becoming. Then a little nudge came over me. Before you proceed to the next chapter, grab your journal and answer the writing prompts.

9

CREATE WITH FAITH

"Now faith is the substance of things hoped for, the evidence of things not seen."
—Hebrews 11: 1

It's the beginning of Fall, and it's a sunny day in LA. I'm sitting at a restaurant on the phone with my mom crying again. I'm sure by now you've determined I'm a sensitive crybaby. This time, I'm not crying about another obstacle that I was working my way through. I wished that was the case. I was crying about this nudge that I couldn't ignore anymore. It was telling me to quit my job and start the Go for Yours Foundation. I couldn't begin to stomach the thought of encountering some of the same obstacles I had in Chicago. This time, I didn't have granny's basement in Chicago to fall back on. There were real bills and responsibilities involved.

Why would God tell me to quit when I loved my job and the stability, I had worked so hard to have? I was back on track and living the conventional/fabulous life that I was still seeking. But I had to answer a new call from God. Despite my nervousness, I knew it was something I had to do.

My mom and I prayed and agreed that I would be obedient to what I felt God was telling me to do. Again, I decided to leave a full-time job, but I prepared in advance this time.

At the beginning of 2018, I started working full-time for the Go for Yours Foundation, whose mission is to provide the next generation of leaders with financial assistance, resources, and mentorship to make a difference in their communities. I created the foundation's initiatives after witnessing students attending schools in impoverished communities not receiving the same resources as their privileged peers. They were talented but didn't have access to the same opportunities. That bothered me. My vision for the foundation is to help close the opportunity gap for underserved youth.

The flagship programs and services are the Go for Yours fund and the Dream Experience. The Go for Yours Fund is a scholarship for young artists, entrepreneurs, and innovators who need financial assistance to achieve their dreams. My inspiration behind it was a young lady who had dreams of competing in the Olympics for swimming. Although she was on the high school swim team, she needed additional training to compete at the Olympic level. Because she couldn't afford the classes, she starting to lose sight of her dream. These are the types of problems many underprivileged children face. They have goals but no resources to fund them. The Go for Yours Foundation was created to help solve this problem.

I had no idea how the money would be raised; I just knew something had to happen so the foundation could begin making a difference in young people's lives. I just moved forward in planning the initiatives. The answer to my prayers of bringing in funds came through my good friend, Paige Simpson. She shared with me the idea of taking a group of students to see *Black Panther.* Paige believed if we created something, she could get celebrities involved and recruited me because she was not familiar with nonprofit foundations and how they worked. Without hesitation, I agreed to work with Paige to put a fundraiser together. We would raise money for kids to see *Black Panther,* and the remainder of the proceeds would go to the Go for Yours fund. Initially, we were planning to raise money for youth residing in Los Angeles only. After speaking to potential funders, we added Atlanta to the list and, of course, Chicago.

Paige, myself, and our friend Justin Key created a campaign to raise money to send students to see *Black Panther.* We got all our friends involved in donating and received additional support from celebrities, including Usher Raymond, whose foundation we ended up partnering with for the Atlanta event. Someone even made a $700 donation after actor/activist Jesse Williams tweeted about our fundraiser. A lot of people and organizations sent students to see *Black Panther,* but ours made national headlines. The Go for Yours Foundation was featured in *Forbes Magazine Online and Rolling out Magazine Online.*

God's favor was with me every step of the way. While creating a list of people to invite to the LA kick-off screening, I met with a Development Consultant who suggested I reach out to Tina Knowles-Lawson and her nonprofit foundation. With us being less than a week away, I told him I would reach out but didn't know if they would be able to come in that short of a time. I had never officially met her, so I had no idea why or how she would come to the foundation's event.

True story. On my way home, I stopped to grab a quick bite to eat. Would you believe it if I told you that Richard Lawson, Mrs. Tina Knowles-Lawson's husband was in the same restaurant? I asked him if he would be interested in bringing students from Tina's Angels and Richard's Warriors to see *Black Panther*. He connected me with the necessary people to make it happen. We had over 200 students and celebrity guests at our opening screening, including Richard Lawson, Tina Knowles Lawson, Kenny Lattimore, and one of the *Black Panther* cast members, Winston Duke! Talk about crazy faith. The *Black Panther* fundraiser helped get the Go for Yours Foundation on its feet and become visible across the country.

When creating something that God has called you to do, He will show up in ways you can't begin to comprehend. Because I stepped out on a limb, God opened up doors to carry out the purpose He placed inside me. Creating with faith is essential because, without it, you will have a restricted view of what God can do in your life. You won't carry out the vision that He has placed in your heart if you don't have faith. I'm not talking about any kind of faith. I am talking about the type of faith that will make people think you're crazy. It's what you need when you answer God's call.

Think about it; someone with insane faith created all the inventions you see, whether it is the internet, the automobile, or the computer. Anyone who started a significant movement in history strongly believed in something they had yet to see. Martin Luther King's dream broke barriers that helped shape the world we live in today. Some people thought he was crazy, but he moved forward with confidence that he was following God's plan. Harriet Tubman, another person with wild faith. After escaping and finding freedom, people thought she was crazy to want to go back and free more slaves. Harriet escorted over 300 slaves to freedom because she followed a God-given dream. Also, keep in mind there were very few resources during that time. If Harriet can accomplish her dream by following the north star, you can surely follow whatever you set out to accomplish. There are too many resources not to. All and all, the same power that was given to groundbreaking individuals resides in you. It's time to step out on crazy faith.

Due to the expenses from *Black Panther*, there wasn't much left for the Go for Yours Fund. When I returned home from the Atlanta screening, I received a phone call from a lady named Vikki Stokes. She had recently discovered the foundation and contacted me because she was raising money for her son Thelonious. He had been accepted into the Florence Academy of Art in Italy and would be the second African American to attend the school and the first to graduate. Because it was his first year, Thelonious was not able to receive scholarships. His mother started a fundraising campaign and was reaching out to the Go for Yours Foundation for assistance. She had raised the majority of funds and only needed about $1,500 to meet their goal by the end of the week.

I told Vikki that the foundation was low on funds due to the *Black Panther* initiative, but I would see what I could do. Two days later, I woke up with Thelonious and his mother on my mind. Something in my spirit told me to give them $500. I knew it was less than the amount she told me was needed, but I went with my gut feeling.

I called Vikki and asked how the fundraising was going. "*We are at the final stretch; all we need is $500.*" She told me. I couldn't believe my ears. It was so hard to hold back the tears as I said to her that was the exact amount that was placed on my heart to give. It was at that moment that God displayed His ability to show up at the very last minute. Being used at this moment taught me a valuable lesson. You never know how and when your blessing is going to show up. When God calls you to do something, He will provide you with everything you need, even if it's in the final hour.

Just like that, Thelonious became the first recipient of the Go for Yours Fund. Today, he is the first African American to graduate from the Florence Academy of Art in Italy. I get excited about the thought of helping more young people like Thelonious. Hopefully, this story will inspire you to let God use you in a mighty way. Let

God use you to make an influence in the world. Let Him use you to be a blessing to others. Let Him use you to live out the vision He has planned for your life. If I hadn't answered the call when I did, I wouldn't have been on track for one of the biggest miracles I've seen in the foundation to date. I have also realized that answering the call was more about helping others than anything else.

How? What? When? Where? Even with crazy faith, we tend to ask these types of questions. I asked them when trying to figure out how I would bring a cohort of students to Los Angeles from all over the country. I had no idea, but I envisioned it. I even had a name for it, the Go for Yours Dream Experience. It would bring the next generation of youth for a 7-day summer intensive program focusing on leadership development, civic engagement, and entrepreneurship. This wasn't any ordinary program; the Dream Experience would change the narrative for black youth. It sounded great, but I had no idea how it would happen. However, I tapped into my crazy faith and began planning while not having $1 raised toward this project.

I put together a preliminary budget and even went as far as viewing potential locations to house the students. With no idea how it would happen, I kept planning. I found a site through Peerspace that was perfect to host the workshops and set up a tour with the venue's owner. The person showing me the space inquired about my program. He asked if the Dream Experience was for black kids. Being asked by a white man, I didn't know how to respond. So, I gave the safe answer, *"It's mostly for young people of color, but all are welcome."*

He replied, *"I'm the CFO of the Shade Room, and I want to connect you with the founder. She'd love this."* For those of you who may not know, the Shade Room is the number one black-owned independent media company that covers entertainment and celebrity news while reaching over 21 Million followers on Instagram alone. The CFO set up a meeting with the Shade Room's founder, Angelica Nwaundu, another person with crazy faith.

Angelica told me how much she loved my book and wanted to help with the foundation. She had such an amazing spirit and shared some of the stories in *Go for Yours with her team.* To make a long story short, Angelica is the person to help me launch the Go for Yours Dream Experience in 2019 by making a significant contribution that covered the costs of flights, lodging, and meals. If it weren't for her support, we wouldn't have a program.

I have always had a sense of crazy faith without even knowing. It took a level of boldness to pursue some of the things I went after. When you are called to create, you have to move when the spirit says move. Don't ponder too long about how you are going to make things happen. When you align with your purpose, God will provide you with all of the resources you need. In your journal, jot down some ways you can step out into crazy faith.

10

THE CREATIVE PROCESS

Intelligence is creativity having fun.
—Albert Einstein

Hopefully, my personal story has motivated you to carry on with the idea tugging at your heart. For a lot of us, we have ideas, and they sound good, but we don't know where to begin. For others, we know where to start, but have challenges when it relates to staying the course. When COVID-19 became a pandemic, I used this opportunity to work on every creative project that had been incomplete.

One of them being, a book I published with my best friend, *All Good Just a Week Ago*. We completed this project in less than a year. I credit the ability to launch a project in less than a year to the creative process I have subconsciously developed while working on various projects.

The process consists of three phases, with three milestones in each stage. Once I learned how to work through each phase, creating became a natural habit. Let's begin to break down this process.

PHASE 1—THE HONEYMOON

As I shared earlier, in the beginning stages of *Go for Yours*, I had so much enthusiasm that it felt like a new relationship, probably because I was in the honeymoon phase. The honeymoon stage is what gets the ball rolling. This is the phase where you are most passionate about what's in your mind to create. You talk about it to anyone who will listen and can't think of one soul who would not be attracted to what you're about to put into action. The three milestones in this phase are as follows.

BIG IDEA. Anything you create will start with a big idea. I'm sure you've had many ideas that haven't made it past this milestone. I have had several big ideas that didn't make it past this stage. Most people don't make it past this milestone because their big idea isn't something that they are passionate about. They may think it's needed, but not necessarily the person to carry out the task. I think it's a good idea to be able to unsend a text message after it's delivered. I would be happy when someone can make it happen, but I would not try to make that idea a concept. When your big idea enters the honeymoon phase, it means you would like to be the driving force to make this creation happen. *Go for Yours* became my big idea after seeing so many young people with no hope for the future. The environment they lived in made it hard for them to live past a certain age. I wanted to create something relatable that would motivate them to see beyond their current situation.

VISION. In this phase, you think about how the world will be different because you decided to move forward with your big idea. You don't see your big idea with a natural eye. You see beyond creation and daydream about every great thing that will happen because you decided to answer the call. Failure isn't even in your thoughts. All you can think about is what will happen when this vision comes to fruition. *I began to imagine all the people whose lives would be impacted because of Go for Yours.*

CONCEPTION. Similar to the conception process that brought all of us to life, when you hit this phase, it means you begin taking steps to bring your big idea to life. You don't have everything you need but use everything you have to get the ball rolling and are committed to learning as you go. The honeymoon stage is a good phase because you are focusing on God's promise for you. In this stage, I began writing and formulating my ideas that would eventually turn into a book.

PHASE 2—REALITY CHECK

The reality check is the most challenging phase, but if you can learn how to maneuver through it, you will be well equipped to complete any task. If you've made it to this phase, it means you have a vision, and you are aware of what you need to get your big idea off the ground.

SECOND GUESSING. The dream you were once fascinated with now has become your biggest nightmare. I've gone through this stage many times in my life. Hence the reason it took me a while to step out on faith. In this milestone of second-guessing, frustration begins to set in, and your vision becomes blurry. You begin to question yourself on why you even thought this was a good idea. Depending on the severity of your frustration, you may consider putting your dream on hold or quitting altogether.

NEW IDEAS. "It's not me; it's the big idea" is what you subconsciously tell yourself during this phase. If you are a creator at heart, you won't throw in the towel; you will just come up with another big idea. In this phase, you begin to think about other ideas that would make more sense to execute. I've been through this phase plenty of times, and although I've had some unexpected detours, I'm always brought back to where God wants me to be. When your big idea doesn't seem so realistic, you may explore new ideas that seem "easier." When you reach this step, pray about whether or not you should be focusing on something new. If it's time for a new idea, just know that you will reach this phase with your next project. So, figure out whether or not it's worth going back to the drawing board. If the answer is no, start thinking of new ideas to keep your vision going. For example, when I was approached with obstacles after writing *Go for Yours*, I thought the answer to my problem was to put it aside and go back to a traditional job. When I saw this was not the answer, I began to think of creative ways to grow my vision and brand.

RELIEF. You've second-guessed and explored other ideas. Now you can finally breathe because you decided to keep your head in the game. The best way to make it through this milestone is by focusing on the promise and not the problem. We face many issues during the reality check phase because we view our obstacles with our natural eye instead of a spiritual one. The thing we're encountering makes our vision blurry. Focusing solely on the problem only creates more problems and tension. When you put your eyes on the God who gave you the promise, you will be able to navigate gracefully through the obstacles. Take a deep breath and move on to the final phase.

PHASE 3—THE FINAL STRETCH

The best way to describe the final stretch is to call it a roller coaster ride. One moment you're up, and the next moment you're down, then up again. If it's not obstacles directly related to your project, then it's personal obstacles. On the bright side, phase 2 prepared you for the final stretch, and there's no turning back. Keep pushing because on the other side of those obstacles is a miracle.

MORE OBSTACLES. Every time I'm about to do something on a large scale, I get hit with something that impacts me personally. Two weeks before the Go for Yours Dream Experience, I went through a personal battle that made my vision very blurry. Instead of spending time working on my project, I began to tend to my problem. When I started to focus on the very thing that God wanted me to focus on, there was no turning back. If it's not a personal problem, then it's something like my computer crashing right before I published *Go for Yours* making me lose most of my material.

PERSEVERANCE. I often call this milestone the third trimester or the final push because your baby that was conceived in phase one is about to be born. Nothing will stop you once you've reached this moment. You're almost at the finish line, and you feel like you did in the honeymoon phase again but even better. You are no longer intimidated by any bump in the road. Some of you will be so enthusiastic about this stage that you won't sleep until your project is complete. The adrenaline you have is even greater than the honeymoon phase. Even if you're tired, you will do whatever it takes to see your baby come to life.

FRUITION. Congratulations! You made it to the finish line, and you have a new creation on deck. It wasn't so bad, was it? You are too happy to even think about all of the things you endured that led to the finish line. You're just ready to change the world with the masterpiece you've created. Go to your Don't Wait Create journal to reflect on a time you subconsciously went through all phases.

11

DON'T WAIT CREATE MODEL

There is no doubt that creativity is the most human resource of all.
Without creativity, there would be no progress, and we would be
forever repeating the same patterns.
—Edward de Bono

To help you navigate the three phases of creating your epic project, I have developed a model that will jumpstart your idea and get you headed to the finish line. In addition to utilizing it for my projects, I use what I now call the Don't Wait Create model to coach creators to the finish line. They have credited this model to helping their big idea become a reality. It's a simple model that allows your vision to become more practical. Grab your journal, and work on the model highlighted on the next page.

- In the circle, jot down your big idea.
- In the box on the top left, write down what experiences you have that make you qualified

to be the facilitator of your big idea. If you don't have any experience, that's okay. Instead, write why you are passionate about this idea. In a lot of cases, passion trumps experience.

- In the resources available box, write down every resource you currently have to help you reach your goal.
- List the resources needed to accomplish your goal in the bottom left box.
- Write down at least three things you can do to start working on your big idea in the next steps box.

The Importance Of This Model

Habakkuk 2:2 tells *us, "write the vision and make it plain."* The big idea helps you get your idea out of your head. Writing your vision down is one of the first steps in conceptualizing your project. Seeing it on paper makes it feel more attainable. It will also help you expand on your ideas as your vision begins to grow.

Often times, we back out on our ideas because we don't feel qualified to achieve them. One of the most incredible things about answering God's call is, you don't need years of experience. Lack of experience is what allows God to do His job as a miracle worker. Don't get discouraged if you lack experience. That's what the next steps are for. If you have knowledge or expertise to help you with your big idea, write down what it is. If you don't, write down what made you develop this idea and why you are the right person to execute it. The purpose of this exercise is to help you feel confident in your ability to bring your vision to life.

There are so many resources available to you. It's time to discover them. Writing down what you need is just as important as writing down your vision. It makes you feel like what you need is possible to obtain. Knowing what you need is valuable when asking for help. There have been times when I needed help but didn't know what to ask for because I didn't know exactly what I needed.

When you take inventory of your experiences, identify your resources, and understand what you need, you are in a better position to create a roadmap to execute your big idea successfully. If I hadn't moved forward in my next steps, I might not have a successful program for my foundation. Creating next steps helped me begin to plan effectively to make it to the creative process's last milestone. It will do the same for you. To help you gain a better understanding, I have provided you with a couple of examples on the next page on charts A & B.

CHART A

EXPERIENCE

None
(Passion)

RESOURCES AVAILABLE

- Computer
- Internet
- Seed Money

BIG IDEA

Go for yours
(Book)

RESOURCES NEEDED

- GraphicDesigner
- Editor

NEXT STEPS

- Create Outline
- Develop Story Concept
- Reach out to people to interview
- Create Facebook Page

CHART B

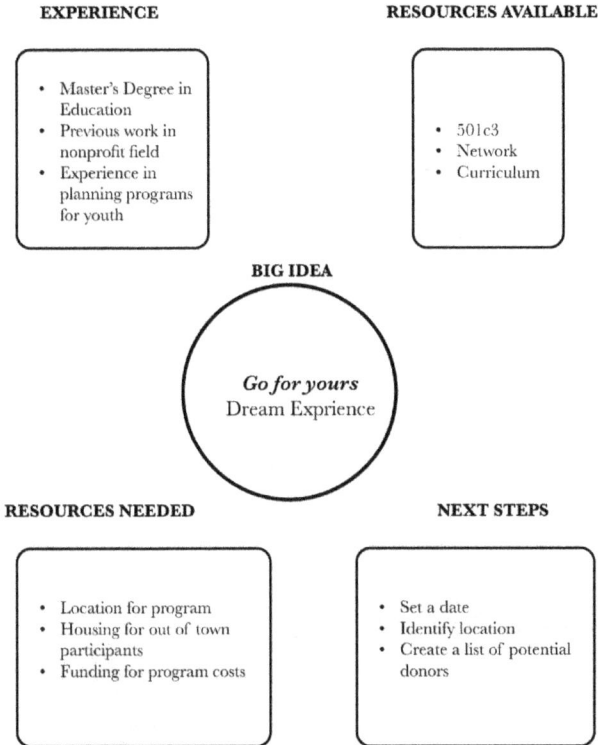

EXPERIENCE

- Master's Degree in Education
- Previous work in nonprofit field
- Experience in planning programs for youth

RESOURCES AVAILABLE

- 501c3
- Network
- Curriculum

BIG IDEA

Go for yours
Dream Exprience

RESOURCES NEEDED

- Location for program
- Housing for out of town participants
- Funding for program costs

NEXT STEPS

- Set a date
- Identify location
- Create a list of potential donors

Chart A

Big Idea: Go for Yours (Book)

Description of Big Idea: *Go for Yours* is a guide for ambitious, faithful, and progressive individuals who seek to break the conventional models of living. It will feature young trailblazers who were brave enough to follow their dreams.

Experience: I didn't have any experience in this area, so instead, I will share why I am passionate about this project.

- There aren't enough books about progressive black people that are relatable to young people.
- Young people are losing hope.
- I've always wanted to write a book, and to me, this is a great idea

Resources Available

- Laptop (to write a book)
- Internet (for research)
- Money (for publishing costs)

Resources Needed

- Publishing Company (to publish the book)
- Graphic Designer (to design book cover)
- Editor (to edit book)

> Creating a description of my big idea helped me gain a better understanding of my vision.

Next Steps

- Create an outline of the book
- Develop story concepts

- Reach out to people to conduct interviews

CHART B

Big Idea: Go for Yours Dream Experience

Description of Big Idea: The Go for Yours Dream Experience is a Summer Fellowship for the next generation of leaders. Participants will fly to Los Angeles (the city of dreams) for a one-week program that focuses on leadership development, entrepreneurship, and civic engagement.

Experience:

- Master's Degree in Adult & Higher Education.
- Previous work in the nonprofit field.
- Experience in working with youth.

Resources Available

- 501c3 nonprofit Foundation.
- Access to entrepreneurs that can help with programming.

> It's not necessary, but creating an outline of your Don't Wait, Create chart will help your stay organized and on task.

- Relationships with individuals that can help make this happen.

Resources Needed

- Location for program
- Housing for out of town participants
- Funding for program costs

Next Steps

- Set a date for program
- Identify location
- Begin fundraising

THE ORGANIZED CREATOR

For every minute spent in organizing, an hour is earned.
—Benjamin Franklin

When you operate with your brain's creative side, it can be hard to organize your thoughts. The ideas that crowd your mind can be quite overwhelming, making it difficult to prioritize. Some creators stay in the reality check phase because they have so many ideas. Their only obstacle is wanting to execute them all at the same time. If this is you, I challenge you to choose one idea to master. Once you've completed one, the rest will be easy to launch. If you are one of the creative people I just described, I recommend going with your best idea. As you make your way towards the finish line, the following tips are helpful during and after the creative process.

Set a deadline and create a task list. Now that you

have an idea of your next steps, it's time to select the desired date for your project to be complete. With a deadline in mind, you will be able to operate even if your vision becomes blurry due to the bumps in the road. Your task list will help you move through your next steps and identify other necessities to help you reach your goal.

Prioritize. There's a difference between being productive and busy. Productivity produces results while being busy does the exact opposite. Don't let your project get you caught up in unnecessary tasks. This is where working smart comes in to play. Yes, you will have to put in hard work, but make sure it's towards something that will produce fruit. If you can identify which tasks need immediate attention, it will alleviate stress.

Create a timeline for each task. A timeline is one of the best ways to track your progress without feeling like you have to complete everything in one day. There are many resources at your fingertips to help you project manage your goals. You can start with a pen and some paper. Or better yet, your Don't Wait, Create journal.

Along with setting timelines, make a list of 1-3 tasks you can fulfill daily. You will feel accomplished as you progress. Whenever I have a day that doesn't seem productive, I ask myself what I need to get done to feel accomplished. Even if it's just one thing, I am still moving forward. So, if I need to take a break, I don't feel so bad.

Delegate. There will come a time when you will not be able to execute every task on your own. In the next chapter, we will talk about creating your dream team. If you don't have a dream team, there are ways to outsource at low costs—one of my favorites is Fiverr. I have used this app to get logos created, find editors and people to format my book. Organizing your task list and timeline will help you identify what can be handed off to someone else.

Create a business, strategic, or marketing plan. As discussed early, I highly encourage you to create a plan. For some of you, it may be all three. It doesn't need to be long. Just something to help guide you along the way. Put some thought into where you want to take your creation.

PUTTING IT INTO ACTION

In your journal, write down the date you want your masterpiece to be complete. Make a list of everything that needs to be done to reach the final milestone of creation. Next, prioritize what's most important. Lastly, create a timeline for each task. Keep in mind that your goals, timelines, and even launch date may change. The importance is tracking your progress. Here's an example using some of the steps I used for this book.

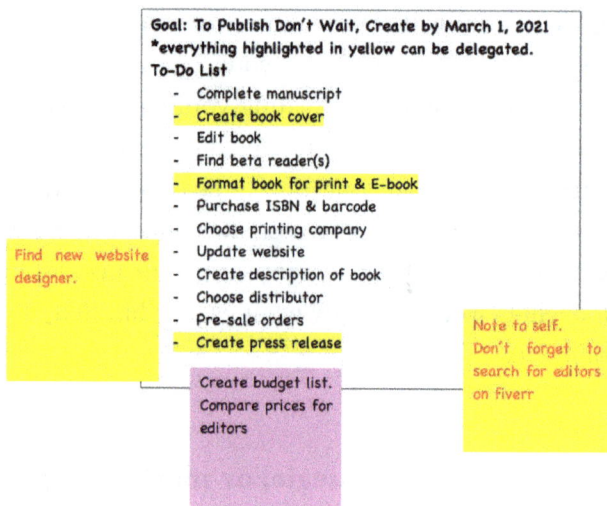

Goal: To Publish Don't Wait, Create by March 1, 2021
*everything highlighted in yellow can be delegated.
To-Do List
- Complete manuscript
- Create book cover
- Edit book
- Find beta reader(s)
- Format book for print & E-book
- Purchase ISBN & barcode
- Choose printing company
- Update website
- Create description of book
- Choose distributor
- Pre-sale orders
- Create press release

Find new website designer.

Create budget list. Compare prices for editors

Note to self. Don't forget to search for editors on fiverr

In the next example, I prioritized my list by putting each task in order. I made each deadline according to my launch date. If I'm publishing a book in November, everything doesn't need to be complete by March. Your list will continue to grow as other components are added.

To-Do List
PRIORITIZED

1. ~~Choose distributor (November 1)~~
2. ~~Choose printing company (December 1)~~
3. Purchase copyright (December 1)
4. Purchase ISBN & barcode (December 1)
5. ~~Hire (December 15)~~
6. ~~Find beta readers (December 15)~~
7. Complete manuscript (January 15)
8. Send manuscript to editor (January 15)
9. Create description of book (February 1)
10. Book Cover complete (February 1)
11. ~~Complete marking plan (February 15)~~
12. Send manuscript to book formatter (February 1)
13. Create press release (February 1)
14. Publish book (March 1)

Note to self. Contact Jack from distribution company.

Update budget & expenses.

Find beta readers on Fiverr. Interview editors by Friday.

Incorporating your list into your daily life can be a task within itself. The example list is just a snapshot into the life of a creator with other priorities. Creating deadlines and adding them to your calendar will help you move forward in your goals as you meet your current life demands. Since this is in book format, I can only give you a small example of what a creator's calendar looks like. In my electronic calendar, I schedule times to complete my tasks. First, I will break my calendar down by the month, then give you an example of how I incorporate my project tasks. If you're writing a book, you've been provided a few tips, so get that book off the ground!

FEBRUARY 2021

SUNDAY	MON	TUES	WED	THURS	FRI	SAT
	1	2	3	4	5	6
	Book Cover & description	90-minute coaching session	Court Reporting		Manuscript edits	
7	8	9	10	11	12	13
Start 28-day workout challenge	Work on marketing plan	Court Reporting	Final Edits	15-minute consultation	Writing Day	
14	15	16	17	18	19	20
Valentine's Day ;)	Marketing plan due	Court Reporting	Client meeting	Meeting	Fun day	Beach day
21	22	23	24	25	26	27
	Schedule social media posts		Meet with interns.	Board Meeting	Writing Day	
28						

Don't forget to create content for website.

Update paperwork for foundation.

Breaking down the week

MON	TUES	WED	THURS	FRI
-Create book cover, write bio, and contact distributor	-Look up printing companies -Make a list of top three	-Contact Distribution companies	- Contact Printing Companies	-Edit chapters one and two - Complete final chapter

*pay phone bill (2/17)
*Schedule team meeting

*Make grocery list for meal prep

Hopefully, this chapter gives you a glimpse of what it looks like to be an organized creator. In your journal, you have been provided with exercises to help you begin the process of becoming more organized. I highly suggest purchasing a calendar or using an electronic one.

13

CHARACTERISTICS OF A CREATOR

A successful creator not only developed habits that are helpful for their overall success. They have tremendous integrity, and their characteristics make them stand out among the crowd. Some of the patterns you acquire will depend on your creative style. For instance, when writing a manuscript, I write my ideas down on paper, type them out, edit, and then repeat. Some people type everything out on the computer and edit from there. Both habits can lead to a finished product. Then there are traits you must have if you want to create and elevate. A lack of these habits can be detrimental to your success. They are as follows.

Consistency. Many people don't make it beyond the honeymoon phase because they fail to work consistently toward their goal. I know it's considered the opposite of sanity, but sometimes the best way to reach your destination is to do the same thing over and over again until you achieve your goal. For example, if someone wants to work out, they will work out and eat healthy repeatedly. Of course, they will change some of their workouts and eating plans to reach their goal, but in essence, they create some form of consistency to make it to the finish line.

Be prepared for your moment. I often have this recurring dream where I am in a room with an important individual. We are in a deep conversation, and I tell them about my book, *Go for Yours*. When they ask for a copy, I don't have one with me. I scramble in my purse for my keys and head to my car, hoping to find one in the trunk. I find a copy, but by the time I return, that person is nowhere in sight. Dreams like this keep me on my toes. I'm sure you've heard it a time or two, *"luck is when preparation meets opportunity."* The best thing you can do for your dream is to be prepared. Your level of preparation depends on what it is you are trying to accomplish. In your *Don't Wait, Create Journal,* make a list of things you need to do that will help you prepare for your moment. Here are some ways to be ready for your opportunity.

Have something tangible to show when an opportunity comes your way. Don't just talk about it, be about it. I'm not saying you have to carry your book or mixtape everywhere you go. But, if someone asks for a snippet of your work, you should have something tangible to send. If not, don't talk about it. Hold off until you are ready with something to present.

Have your elevator pitch ready. We live in a world where people are always in a rush. Have a 30 second or less description ready when talking to people about your business or brand. Make sure it's catchy. The goal is to land an extended conversation or meeting.

Gain knowledge about the industry you are trying to break into. Whether it is in the classroom or through experience, make sure you gain as much knowledge and education about whatever it is you are striving to do. There is nothing worse than landing an opportunity and not knowing how to fulfill the role.

Maximize your moments. When taking a cycling class one morning, the instructor encouraged the class to make the very best out of their workout. He reminded us that we only had 45 minutes to give it our all. Although it was a tough 45 minutes, we would be happy with the results. This can easily apply to your dream. Take advantage of every moment. There are some moments you may not get back.

Be kind to people. You are probably wondering, what does being kind to people have to do with being prepared? You would be surprised how many doors have opened for me just because I am kind. How you treat others can take you a long way. Treating people with respect and dignity will make them want to work with you over a more talented person with a bad attitude.

Make room for your blessing. The best way to make room for the new is to get rid of the old. It could be old habits, old mindsets, relationships, and even old items in your house. It's hard to embrace something new if you are still holding on to things that no longer serve you.

CREATE EXPERIENCE

One of the many characteristics of a creator is the ability to find new experiences. Creating experiences is helpful if you are looking to break into a new field or start a business. One of the best ways to gain experience is through internship and volunteer opportunities. You never know what type of doors they will open. A volunteer opportunity is what ultimately brought me to the West Coast. Internships and volunteer opportunities are the perfect time to expand your network and show off exceptional skills that will make people inquire about you. Giving your time will sew a positive seed into the work you desire to do. When creating experiences, utilize them in a way that is effective for you. When providing your services for free or at a low cost, here are a few tips.

Make sure it is a learning opportunity. This is especially true for interns. Do not give your time to an internship that just wants you to fetch coffee or run errands. A good internship will make sure your experience aligns with your career goals.

Volunteer to expand your network. A great thing about volunteering is that it allows access to places you may not have been able to get into on your own. When you have completed your tasks, you can interact with individuals and fellow volunteers, leading to authentic connections.

Get to know your fellow volunteers and interns. Don't just hobnob with the folks who you deem to be elite. People who volunteer are usually professionals with similar dreams. Together, you can provide each other with resources that will help along your journey.

Put in the work. Don't volunteer just because you want to get into an event or program. Get your hands dirty and fulfill the tasks that are required. Being genuine about the reason you are helping will get you to exactly where you need to be.

. . .

Don't allow yourself to be taken advantage of.
Some people love taking advantage of a hungry go-getter. Don't fall into the trap. Ensure you are getting out as much as you are putting into your role as a volunteer or intern.

Know when it's time to get paid. Free work should always have a deadline attached to it. After all, you have to make a living. Don't be afraid to ask for compensation. If there is not a budget large enough to pay you, seek another opportunity.

CREATE AN OPPORTUNITY, NOT AN OPPORTUNIST

OPPORTUNIST (noun)
    A person who exploits circumstances to gain immediate advantage rather than being guided by consistent principles or plans.

———————

While on the topic of character, I would be remiss if I didn't point out the difference between creating an opportunity and being an opportunist. A person who is an opportunist has motives that leave people wanting to flee anytime they come in their direction. During my journey, I met many people who come off as opportunists instead of people who genuinely want to create an opportunity. Here are some characteristics of an opportunist.

They ask someone to listen to their demo, read their script, or hand out their resumé at the wrong time and place. I remember being at an event attended by Snoop Dogg. This lady followed him around, singing loud in hopes that he would notice her. I've never witnessed someone looking so desperate for attention. Be mindful of the place and time you are creating an opportunity. God's plan for your life will never steer you off course. You will connect with the right people at the right time.

They ask people who don't know them to be introduced to their agent or manager in hopes they will represent them. Doing this is like asking someone to be a reference or write a recommendation that doesn't have any idea about you or your work ethic. I recommend you develop a relationship before asking anyone for a reference.

They abuse crowdfunding campaigns for something they have the ability to fund. Think of creative ways to raise capital for your business. Utilize resources like Go Fund Me and Kickstarter as a way to strengthen your brand or help someone in need. If you want people to take you seriously, try to refrain from creating multiple fundraising campaigns asking for people's hard-earned money while providing nothing in return.

They befriend certain people because of their connections. I have encountered plenty of people around me only because of the people I know. They are easy to identify, and when I do, I stay away from them. Make sure you are genuine about the connections you make.

They approach people at places like the grocery store, restaurant, or church, trying to connect with them. Allow people to live their regular life. If you see someone you want to connect with trying to enjoy personal time, it's okay to say hello and introduce yourself, but try not to go further than that.

They are all talk and no action. These are the worst kind. You never want to appear to be that person who talks a good game but has nothing to bring to the table.

They overpromise and under-deliver. Like people who are all talk, these people try to sell a dream to lock down an opportunity instead of being honest with what they can deliver.

They name drop. This type of opportunist always talk about who they know, but not many people know them. If they do, it's for all of the wrong reasons. It's okay to be ambitious, but you never want to look like that desperate opportunist. A person who creates a genuine opportunity isn't pressed because they are confident that they possess something the world needs. They know their time to shine is coming.

Ways To Create Genuine Opportunities

Always present yourself in the best light. When you professionally carry yourself, people will notice you. You won't have to go through desperate measures to get their attention because they will want to know who you are. Be confident in knowing you will be able to showcase your talent at the appropriate place and time.

Be professional in your approach. When you do get a chance to connect with someone, introduce yourself and give your elevator pitch. Ask them if you can send them an email and connect with them at a later date.

. . .

Show people rather than tell them. Remember, you hold more value when people ask about you. Keep skillfully doing your work and be ready for the opportunities when they come to you. Creating an opportunity does not mean you have to chase it.

Under-promise and over-deliver. This is a great strategy I learned after moving to LA. Even if you know you can do fantastic work, let the people know what you can do at a minimum. Anything else will be a bonus.

Your character will play a massive role in your success. In what ways do you model integrity in your work? Have you ever modeled the characteristics of an opportunist? If so, how?

14

CREATE YOUR DREAM TEAM

"Teamwork makes the dreamwork, but a vision becomes a nightmare when the leader has a big dream and a bad team."
—John C. Maxwell

I t would have been impossible for Michael Jordan to work his magic without his coach Phil Jackson and his teammates, Scottie Pippen, Horace Grant, and my favorite basketball player of all time, BJ Armstrong. Building a team that can help execute your vision is essential to your success as a creator.

From the very beginning, I have been blessed with individuals who have helped grow my vision. Starting with my line sister Tiara, who was the first editor of *Go for Yours*, and my soror Tonja who helped me create my social media pages. My very first intern, Jamie, played a considerable role in helping me gain visibility on campus.

Today, my dream team is full of talented people, including Candace, another college friend, and soror who uses her passion for Event Planning to build the brand. My cousin Marcus helped launch my publishing company, and my cousin Neidra helps with social media. My team also consists of the Go for Yours Foundation board members and Go for Yours Ambassadors. Everyone I mentioned works just as hard as I do, if not harder. They are knowledgeable areas that I am not strong in.

Most of the people I mentioned above are volunteers or charge a low rate because they understand and believe in my vision. I'm often asked how I attract such amazing people. The following tips will help you build your dream team.

Find out what your team members are most passionate about. Before adding anyone to my team, I find out about their goals. I ask them to share with me their plans for their professional career. This shows them that I care about their career goals.

Ask how working with you will help them achieve the goals mentioned above. I want to make sure that I help contribute to the professional goals of the people who are helping me. If I am not able to pay them, the least I can do is help them win.

Create a position or tasks that allow them to use their skills while contributing to your

business. After hearing about their goals and how I can help, I create a position that will enable them to carry out meaningful tasks that can serve as a resume builder.

Make them a part of your vision. When it comes to creating, I encourage my dream team members to join in on the vision. When you create something larger than yourself, you have to figure out ways to connect people to your vision. When you make people feel connected to what you're doing, they will execute with greatness.

Show appreciation. This is important. I know what it feels like to be unappreciated. After working with leaders who did not show gratitude, I make it a habit of letting people know that I value their services.

Empower them. Leaders empower people to be great. They don't use scare tactics to make them get the work done. Real leaders connect with their team members and encourage them to be the best person they were created to be.

VIBE WITH YOUR TRIBE:

"Friends don't let friends dream alone."
—Donald George, Comedian

TRIBE *(noun)*

The people that will be there for you no matter what and who you're guaranteed to have a good time with. Although people may not understand how close they are and their relationships with each other, it doesn't matter because they all understand it and love one another.

As an entrepreneur, I spend a lot of time in front of my laptop or at a business meeting. I have built a strong professional network, but it's the interactions with my friends and family that provide me with the extra boost I need to keep pushing. They are my sounding board when I am going through tough times and a shoulder to cry on when I'm having a bad day. We have fun together, travel together, and follow our dreams together. The people in my tribe are a constant reminder that I am not alone in my journey.

During his comedy shows, Donald George often wears a shirt that says, *"friends don't let friends dream alone."* I met Donald through my friend and neighbor, Darryl Dunning. I have to say; they live by this mantra. Whether they are attending one of his comedy shows, a screening of one of Darryl's films, celebrating our friend Taurus' birthday, or supporting another friend's project, you can see that they support each other's dreams.

The members of my tribe are a constant reminder that we are in this together. I met one of the sweetest, funniest, and loyal friends I have ever encountered in college. She always tells me, *"everyone needs an Erika in their life."* I believe that everyone needs a Niesha in their life. She is one of my biggest cheerleaders.

We all meet people who say they are our friends, but they are nowhere to be found when approached with a problem. I knew Niesha was different when I became sad after a breakup. She called on a Friday night to see if I wanted to go out. I declined because my funds were low. Niesha insisted I come over to her house. When I arrived, she had a stylish outfit with $50 waiting for me on the bed. This gesture took my understanding of friendship to a new level. It wasn't the money or even the outfit. Her small act of kindness showed me that she had my back no matter what. She wanted me to know what I was experiencing wouldn't last forever, and she believed in me. Niesha and I continue to support each other's dreams. We still talk every day, and I couldn't be prouder of her for starting her own business, *Compass Vintage*, an online vintage boutique specializing in finding items from around the world and bringing them straight to your closet. We even wrote a book together called *All Good Just a Week Ago*. In case you haven't checked it out, it's a book of funny dating stories to help you keep your head in the game.

Another friend I hold near and dear to me is when

my good friend Jimmy Prude and founder of Jimmy's Vegan cookies (another shameless plug), invited me to dinner for his birthday. I was almost done writing *Go for Yours* and was on the financial struggle bus. I hesitated at first because I didn't want to attend a group dinner with me being broke. You never know what will happen when the bill comes. Nonetheless, I scraped up a few dollars to celebrate my good friend's birthday downtown.

When the bill came, Jimmy leaned over to me and whispered, *"I can pay for yours if you need me to."* This small gesture of my friend wanting to pay for me on his birthday warmed my heart. It's friends like these that help me move on in the midst of obstacles. A huge part of your accomplishments will come from creating a well-rounded support system that consists of great friends and family. . Having people who genuinely care for your well-being is worth more than any amount of success you can obtain.

CREATE WITH ENERGY FROM YOUR LOVED ONES

"When you walk into an office, you don't go alone. Bring your people with you, bring everybody who has loved you with you."
—Maya Angelou

Maya Angelou gave this piece of advice years ago while giving her commencement address at Spelman College. When she says, "bring your people with you," she was not referring to bringing them in a physical sense. Metaphorically speaking, she was saying bring their energy with you. When you walk into a room knowing you already have people who care about you, it increases your confidence and brings light to you that will leave people wondering where it came from.

My transition to Los Angeles left me experiencing some growing pains I was not ready for. Being in a new city and job often left me filled with anxiety. With the fear of failure weighing on me heavily, there were times when I couldn't sleep because the thought of failure made me feel miserable. My relationship with the people who supported me the most is what prevented me from giving up. It was their love and support that sustained me. Whenever I am faced with a challenging task, I find confidence knowing that I have people in my life who genuinely love and support me. Whether it's an important meeting, an interview, or even a date, I take the energy of my loved ones with me. So, when I encounter ingenuine people, I am reminded of their love.

I understand everyone may not have these types of relationships. Even if you do, the love from family and friends may not always be enough. This is why it's so important to understand God's love. To know that God loved me enough to create me is a feeling I take with me everywhere I go. Create energy from the people who love you, including God's love.

One person's energy that I always take with me is my sister Tiffany. My journey has allowed me to meet people I have looked up to for years.

Excited about who I connected with, I would often call my sister and tell her about my latest interaction. Her immediate response would be, "so, you are Erika

McCall!" Meaning, she believes I'm just as important as the people I encountered. Sometimes she would add a few choice words between my first and last name to remind me how important she thinks I am. Every time I head back to LA after visiting my family, Tiffany tells me, "remember, you are Erika McCall!" before sending me on my way. Most recently, she sent me a text that read, "you are a child of God, you are THEE ERIKA RESHANDA MCCALL, and don't forget it." I am so grateful for my sister because she never wants me to forget the value I bring to the table. With support like this, how can I lose?

In the world we live in, people will quickly make you feel less than you are. You will come across people who will try to steal your joy and self-esteem like a thief in the night. When I walk into rooms, I always remember that I am Erika Reshanda McCall—taking with me the energy of everyone who loves me. Start thinking about the people who love you the most. It could be your parents, grandparents, siblings, friends, children, or significant other. When approaching new territory, bring their energy with you remembering who you are! Now say it with me, *"I am (insert name), the next (fill in the blank)!"* Now write this in your journal.

DESTINY HELPERS

A few weeks before moving to Los Angeles, I met a young lady from London by the name of Elizabeth. Although we lost touch, I will forever remember the conversation we had about people coming into our lives as "destiny helpers." These are the people who help you along the way during your journey. Some of them may be members of your tribe, while others are there for a particular moment in time. To say I accomplished everything on my own would be disrespectful to all of the people who have supported me along the way. Each destiny helper I crossed paths with has played a significant part in me living out my dreams.

Two destiny helpers played a significant role in me moving to Los Angeles. The first being my good friend Akello Stone affectionately known as Kell. He was the Executive Director for the foundation I ended up moving to California for. It's him who initially saw something in me when I was just a volunteer. He was the person who saw my talent and advised Hill to take a call with me. Kell is the destiny helper that played a role in my new chapter in Los Angeles. It was his belief in me that made the founder want to learn more about who I was. For that, I am forever grateful. He is also one of the reasons I ended up being the Executive Director. After leaving his day job, he chose to seek opportunities that would allow him to create what was in his heart to do. One of them being his book titled *Seeking Selfdom in the Age of Selfies*.

Another destiny helper who played a significant role is my good friend and sorority sister Jarquetta Egeston. During my first interview for the position in LA, I was so nervous that I offered to plan an event for the foundation in Chicago. Hill had recently published *Letters to an Incarcerated Brother*, and I offered to arrange a panel and book signing. I contacted Jarquetta, who was working at Roosevelt University at the time. She provided me with the space to host the program. Through her, I was able to showcase my talent that ultimately led to me being hired.

Destiny helpers are crucial to your success. The unique thing about them is, you don't have to go looking for them. God sends them right on time to help when you need it the most. I will forever be grateful for the plethora of destiny helpers who have supported me along the way. I am even more thankful that I can call most of them my friend. As you meet destiny helpers along the way, keep in mind the importance of being one. Like I said before, we are in this together.

Grab your don't wait create journal and map out your dream team along with your destiny helpers.

15

CREATE YOUR BEST LIFE!

"I'm living my best life. I ain't going back and forth with you people."
—*Smile (I'm living my best life),* Lil Duval

We can thank social media for the cookie-cutter images of what living your best life should look like. Trips out of the country, photos with celebrities, and snapshots of gourmet dishes can make some of us feel like we aren't really living. Your best life is not about creating a highlight reel to make people wish they were as successful as you. It's more about enjoying the life that has been created just for you.

Make fun a priority in your life. Everything doesn't have to be super serious. Your job and whatever you're creating is only one aspect of your life. Don't miss out on some of your best days because you are focused solely on work. Creating a work-life balance can be challenging. Heck, I don't even know if it exists. In some seasons, you will be focused more on work than fun. There are ways to enjoy your life while simultaneously handling your responsibilities.

I can successfully fulfill my tasks because I make it a priority to get the very best out of life. If you are struggling to create a life worth living, here are some tips that have helped me.

Be spontaneous. With it being impossible to plan every detail of your life, be open to the spontaneity of your journey. My greatest moments are the unplanned ones. Some of them were as small as stepping away from my work to see a movie or delaying a flight from New York so I can go to the Hamptons with my best friend to enjoy a nice shindig.

Enjoy your surroundings. For some of us, it's time to take a deep breath and appreciate what we already have. Living your best life involves taking time out to enjoy the pleasant scent of flowers and taking hold of the simple things in life.

Spend time with the people you care about. Enjoy time with the people who love and support you the most. There is nothing worse than neglecting your relationships because you are working too much. Your loved ones are the people who will support you during your journey. Enjoy life with them.

. . .

Create a boundary between you and your work.
As a creator, it's easy to get caught up in the mantra of late nights and early mornings. In my experience, I have learned that being productive has nothing to do with the insane number of hours I work. It has more to do with what I'm doing within those hours. I have created boundaries between myself and work. I don't allow my work to take control of my entire life. I make it a priority not to answer emails or schedule unimportant meetings after a particular time. If I'm enjoying leisure time, I try not to focus on my work. I highly recommend identifying what boundaries you need to create between you and your work so you can live your best life.

Embrace the process. You don't have to do this work; you GET to do it. There's a huge difference. The simple fact that God has called you to do something higher than yourself should make you enjoy what you are creating. Most of us think about what we have to do instead of viewing your work as a blessing that you get to wake up and tend to every day. Don't wait until you reach your destination to live your best life. Your experience becomes more valuable when you learn to enjoy the journey instead of focusing so much on the end goal. The friends you meet along the way, the lessons you learn, and once in a lifetime experiences during the process is what makes it worth following your dream.

. . .

Don't sweat the small stuff. As a naturally sensitive Cancerian woman, it's easy for me to get caught up in things that don't matter. Your journey will be filled with situations and people you disagree with. When this happens, pick your battles and don't let anything disturb your peace.

Do something that would normally scare you. As Eleanor Roosevelt once said, "*do one thing every day that scares you.*" You may be thinking; *I'm following my dream, what could be scarier than that?*" True, but I want you to go the extra mile and think about other things you can do to overcome some of the fears you have.

Enjoy the weekends and holidays. Again, you do not have to work 24-7 to be productive in your work. It's important to step away from your responsibilities for at least 24 hours so you can come back feeling refreshed. During the winter holidays, I suggest taking a couple of weeks off to regroup and jumpstart the upcoming year.

Rest and relax. Remember, even God rested on the 7th day. If you are not getting the proper rest, you are doing yourself and your work a disservice. Working 24-7 doesn't always produce the best results.

. . .

Take 30 days off. I know this may sound insane. When you are in the process of creating, spend some time away. Too much time with your project can harm your creativity. Summertime and holidays are an excellent time to take a break. If you are working a full-time job, take some time away from any additional work. Recently, my friend Tiara took 30 days off work to rejuvenate. She went to Denver, Colorado, for a week and visited some other places in between. She returned to her work feeling refreshed and ready to take on the world.

Don't box yourself in. A huge part of living your best life is stepping away from what you think your life should look like and embracing all your talents. If Lil Duval, who I quoted at the beginning of this chapter, would have pursued comedy only, he wouldn't have a song that debuted number 3 on the Billboard 100. Make sure that you make room for every gift you were blessed with.

You can make progress in your work and enjoy life at the same time. If it's been a while since you've done something fun, I encourage you to put this book down and do something that represents living your best life. Even if it's just inviting friends over for game night, don't let life pass you by because you are so focused on your goals. As long as you take care of your responsibilities, there is no reason not to live your best life. As my Uncle Herbert always says, *"take the joy out of life, don't let life take the joy out of you."*

16

THE WAIT IS OVER

But they that wait upon the Lord shall renew their strength; they shall mount up with wings as eagles; they shall run, and not be weary; and they shall walk, and not faint.
—Isaiah 40:31

The wait is officially over. You've arrived. You have finally made it to the point where you abandon the thinking that kept you from acting on your gift of purpose. Long gone are the days where you wait for someone to give you an opportunity that God has already provided you. It's time to put those genius ideas into motion with your best foot forward. Remember, you are qualified and more than equipped to enter into the next season of your life.

Before our time together comes to an end, I want to leave you with a few last nuggets that will help you welcome the new version of yourself. I found that when I did things in this particular fashion, it was an enjoyable process. I had constant reminders of how much everything was divinely orchestrated, which gave me more joy than I could ever imagine.

Embrace your calling. While prepping for a radio interview, the host asked me what else did I do besides writing books. I responded, "I just write books and run a nonprofit foundation." He quickly advised me to take the "just" out of my vocabulary. It took this conversation to remind me that I was downplaying who I am. I had spent so much time grinding that I didn't realize I am a business owner and a creator who was called to create. Most of all, I am a child of God who has given me the power to be everything he has designed me to be. As soon as I fully embraced my true identity in Christ, I changed my entire atmosphere. You may be wondering what that entailed. I walked entirely into my calling by making small changes in my office space. I purchased a sign that said Go for Yours Foundation | Don't Wait Create LLC and a tiny table for it to sit on. I turned my dining room into a workspace, and on my whiteboard, I wrote three words—writer, artist, creator, with bullet points of my goals.

I won't go into every detail, but the point is, I began to work on my calling as hard as I would for a 9-5 job. Of course, various obstacles arise, but when they do, I tackle them with the mindset of the business owner I am. I challenge you to do the same. Step into your calling and own it.

· · ·

Wait on God. If you wait on anything on your journey of creating, it should be God. There will be times when you will have done everything in your power to move forward in your calling, and things may come at a standstill. Often this is God's way of sitting us down in stillness so He can go ahead of us and clear the way. When you find yourself in this moment, understand there is nothing else you can do but to relax and remember God knows the end to your beginning.

Make room for God's supernatural blessings. God wants to show himself mighty through you. He is like the ultimate 401K and will do far more than match your efforts. Remember, before the womb, He knew you and is well aware that you will meet His expectations. God is a miracle-worker! One of my favorite stories in the Bible is when Gideon defeated the Midianites in the book of Judges. God had him take 300 men instead of thousands. The reason for downsizing Gideon's army was so the only person who could receive the glory for defeating the Midianites was God. If they went with the original number of troops, the army would have accredited their victory to the men who fought in the battle. By defeating the Midianites with only 300 men, the glory could only go to God.

God wants to show himself mighty in your life. That's why He doesn't give you everything you think you need to bring forth the ideas you've been sitting on. Don't waste time worrying about not having enough money or resources and believe that God will open doors that you can't open. It has to look almost impossible for the miracle worker to perform a miracle as He is in the business of doing.

Work while God is working. James 2:14 says, *what does it profit, my brethren if someone says he has faith but does not have works? Can faith save him?"* As creative believers, we can't only depend on our prayers to get us to the finish line. While God is creating an avenue and opening doors for you to share your talent, make sure you are doing your due diligence to focus on every task that is in your control. Always remember during this journey, some doors will be open while others will shut. However, they cannot open or close without God's permission. As long as you are obedient to Him and uphold your end of the project, even you can't stop what God has for you.

Our time in this book has come to an end, but your calling has not. It is a blessing to be here to cheer you on, and I hope that your creativity will be birthed and fruitful. I hope my words have encouraged you to engage in creating incredible masterpieces. I thank God that he has given me the incredible task of inspiring His children to use their gifts and answer His call. I can't wait to hear about all of the works He has done through your abilities and talents. Thank you for staying with me until the end. I won't keep you any further as there is no more time left to delay. As we part, I will do so with just one phrase (actually two) Don't Wait, CREATE—GO FOR YOURS. See you in the next book!

www.ingramcontent.com/pod-product-compliance
Lightning Source LLC
Chambersburg PA
CBHW070452090426
42735CB00012B/2516